Ronda Gorge
& Other Precipices

AIDAN HIGGINS

Ronda Gorge
& Other Precipices

Travel Writing 1956–1989

SECKER & WARBURG
London

First published in Great Britain 1989
by Martin Secker & Warburg Limited,
Michelin House, 81 Fulham Road,
London SW3 6RB

British Library Cataloguing in Publication Data

Higgins, Aidan, *1927–*
Ronda Gorge and other precipices
1. Travel – Biographies
I. Title
910.4'092'4

ISBN 0 436 19597 6

'Images of Africa' was first published in book form
by Calder and Boyars, 1971; 'Berlin Days and Nights'
and 'A Crack in the Distributor Head' first appeared
in *Cara*, March/April 1978, September/October 1986;
'*Sommerspiele*, Munich, 1972' and 'Ronda Gorge and
Other Precipices' in the *London Magazine*, November 1982,
February 1984; 'Autumn in Cómpeta' in the
New Statesman, December 1983; 'The Dogs of Cómpeta'
in *The Writers*, O'Brien Press, 1980; 'Gas in the
Decompression Chamber' in *Cyphers*, no. 18, 1983;
'Past Customs', 'Round Trip' and 'Loose Chippings'
in the *Irish Times*, November 17th, 1976, August 12th, 1977,
September 10th, 1977. 'Motoring with Mr MacAuley',
'The Opposite Land' and 'The Other Side' are previously unpublished.

Contents

For Alannah

The geography of mental travel can't be the same from century to century; the realms of gold move away. They float into the past.

Saul Bellow, *Him With His Foot in His Mouth*

Perhaps the best idea is to imagine a country, but never going there; otherwise you end up writing impressionistic letters to those who stayed at home.

Martin Kluger, Berliner

We changed again, and yet again, and now it was too late and too far to go back, and I went on. And the mists had all solemnly risen now, and the world lay spread before me.

Charles Dickens, *Great Expectations*

Images of Africa

1956–60

PART ONE

. . . I entered the wood; and, with all possible wariness and silence, Friday following close at my heels, I marched till I came to the skirt of the wood, on the side which was next to them, only that one corner of the wood lay between me and them. Here I called softly to Friday, and shewing him a great tree which was just at the corner of the wood, I bade him go to the tree, and bring me word if he could see there plainly what they were doing. He did so, and came immediately back to me, and told me they might be plainly viewed there; that they were all about their fire, eating the flesh of one of their prisoners, and that another lay bound upon the sand, a little way from them, which, he said, they would kill next, and which fired the very soul within me. He told me it was not one of their nation, but one of the bearded men he had told me of, that came to their country in the boat. I was filled with horror at the naming of the white bearded man; and, going to the tree, I saw plainly by my glass a white man, who lay upon the beach of the sea, with his hands and feet tied with flags, or things like rushes, and that he was a European, and had clothes on.

Daniel Defoe, *The Life and Adventures of
Robinson Crusoe*

The Voyage

I

The plunge over the equator. Flying fish sink, porpoises rise, and evening after evening the sun goes down in formations of cloud, furnace-like, dramatic as anything in Doré's illustrations to Dante. The approaches to a new continent. Such lovely leewardings! They must lead somewhere.

Undersized dining-room stewards, Malays, traverse the decks banging out the same tune on their dinner gongs. I've grown tired of the narrow regimen of shipboard life — the repetitive meals, the same dull decks and the same dull company — it's a kind of prison.

The passengers for the most part are Dutch or German, or Afrikaners returning to their homeland. One tall Afrikaner — von Lieres — is returning to Van Rhynsdorp in the Cape after several years studying engineering in Germany. He tells me that in some South African families they send their sons into the police force for a year or so to toughen them up before they take up a career. Before they take up a more respectable career? I ask. He gives me a blank look and smiles; we do not make jokes about the police in South Africa. On the first lap of the tour we will run into him again. I share a cabin with two young Germans — also engineers. Going to German South-west Africa. Strategists.

Among the German contingent there is a family from Berlin. The parents sit close together on deck, stoutly perspiring, handkerchiefs over their heads, calling for beer.

5

They have one son of fourteen; it's mainly on his account that they are going to South Africa. Germany is not for them anymore. Two wars in one lifetime – it's enough.

What is it they fear? Communism. Militant Communism. The Tartar tank-crews with their slit eyes and Mongolian features, their strange leather headgear of the Red Army spear-heads that entered Budapest to crush the Hungarian Uprising, finished them. Emanations from a nightmare. It is this they fear. Soviet tanks manned by Asiatic crews.

So off, then; *pis aller!*

The wife hopes to take up her old profession in Johannesburg. Orthopaedics. The husband too will work. Both have done so all their lives, worked hard, they are not young anymore, but they will work for the future of their son.

The small *Fräulein* in Jay's cabin has her wedding-dress and trousseau with her. Though hardly more than a child, she is going out to German South-west Africa to marry a man she has never seen except in photographs. She is a war-orphan from Hamburg. It's an arranged match.

The first sight of Africa low on the horizon on the port side, a dim white skeleton coast; a mirage that goes.

II

Walvis Bay, in South-west Africa. A barrage of heat. Offal from the ship's kitchen floating astern. Seagulls squall over it, their whiteness reflected in a rainbow trail of oil. From the stagnant greenish waters of the roadstead a stench of putrescence rises, sulphuric acid . . . rotten eggs. A squat white bird resembling a penguin paddles round the stern and one of the crew – an idle Malay – takes pot-shots at it through one of the portholes down by the waterline.

Empty deckchairs, inert in the heat, creak in the sun. The wan-looking bride-to-be is taken ashore on a tender with some of the pale young Germans.

Onshore, a collection of shacks face the sea, the sun

shooting fire off corrugated iron roofs. *Die Waterman* out of Amsterdam, a decaying wharf with figures of African dock labourers parading on it, and beyond them, an excessively long rusty-plated terracotta Russian tanker from the Bering Strait – on these the sun, from almost directly overhead, brings to bear its fierce and implacable rays. Baked littoral and saffron dunes, a reflection of a decayed wharf swimming in mid-air, with figures walking upside down on it – all burn and tremble in the sun.

A local flat-boat comes alongside, and into its capacious and dirty hold black men dressed in rags, with bright-coloured bandannas about their heads, begin offloading cargo, while others wait down in the hold. The passengers, laughing, throw them apples and oranges, like into a bear-pit. The oranges explode down in the hold. Some of the remaining sallow-faced young Germans come with jackets under their arms to gape at the coal-black dockers. After a time the flat-boat sails, laden with cargo, grey-black smoke pumping out of its stack. That side of the ship now seems deserted. Leaning over the rail I imagine I can see sand, fathoms down. I see the reflections of a double tier of bored passengers staring down. Their shadows go down shuddering into the deeper green of the sea, where a shoal of voracious red cannibal fish, like mullet, swim up out of the stench against our kelpy side. They come in dense, resolute shoals. When a fishing line, unbaited, touches the water they take it and one by one are pulled on deck. They lie twitching on the boards where one cannot walk bare-footed; quite soon their vivid colour goes.

This desolate place with its heat and smells, the hyena and lion reek of old Africa – this is Walvis Bay. Sidgewick, author of a beginners' book on astronomy, lived for a time with his girl in a cave up in the hills, and died later of heart thrombosis on a boat on the Seine.

At last this jaunt is nearly over. Tonight we lie to at Walvis Bay.

III

A storm before Capetown. All the ports bolted; the wood-work groaning. The Cape rollers begin. Black sea and waves at night. Nausea. We poor sailors turn in early.

In the morning, the storm has blown itself out, though the sea is still running high. We are into Table Bay, *Die Waterman* approaching its berth. A blinding glare comes off the sea. During the night one of the vague young Germans, wandering about the ship, fell down a companionway, suffered a heart-attack, died of it. He lies now in his white cabin. No one knows anything about him. He is to be buried in Capetown. A collection is started.

Provenance. Iphigenia.

Table Mountain looms over us, balancing on its summit a single cloud. It's a hot day in high summer here. The passengers crowd the rail. A beauty in a black dress, wearing sunglasses, stands alone on the quayside and waves to someone standing beside me.

Prancing airs of the Cape of Good Hope. It's December 20th, 1956.

IV

On December 24th, two engines pull a long line of carriages through the Blaauwberg Mountains, on the Garden Route, travelling from Capetown to East London in the Eastern Province. Wheatlands go right up into the foothills of the mountains, which are lime blue. The horizon seems very far away, bright and luminous. Everything is on a grander scale here – even the swallows are bigger. At Mossel Bay, on an island, a lady in a picture-hat paints at an easel.

Blossom, Le Roux, Zebra, Power, George, the Outeniqua Mountains, the beaches of Wilderness, the inland sea of Knysna, the thick green grass of the ostrich farms, an engineless grain train pulled into a siding and Africans in broken sun-hats unloading sugar-cane.

On Xwartkops River, passing New Brighton location outside Port Elizabeth in the dusk of the evening. Lines and lines of hovels give way to arid land. An internment camp sprawls featureless in the evening dusk.

Nothing can be added and nothing can be taken away. An African shanty-town made up of line upon line of huts, hides and skins, open drains; through this lean cattle wander, mangy curs, ghosts. Most mournful aspect. Where the huts end the barren land begins again.

And in the twilight, clinging high on the wire fence like bats, naked piccaninnies stretch out their hands to the lighted carriage windows that are gliding slowly past, the dining-car passing; themselves the colour of dust, chanting: 'Happy . . . happy . . . happy!' Happy Christmas in South Africa.

December 25th. I wake up. I am on the upper berth. The train has been stationary for hours, out on the veldt. I feel warm air coming in through the carriage window and all along the track the crickets are going like wildfire. Then the long train begins to move again with much banging and colliding of bumpers. Onward from Hex River, Mossel Bay, Plettenberg Bay, to Port Elizabeth, East London, King William's Town by the Amatola Mountains.

The Tour

I

For a whole day now we have been travelling through this landscape of grey-blue militant cactus with no other vegetation, no house, the whole face of the land covered with these things, and nothing else as far as the eye can see, scarcely a blade of grass.

We pass an immense dam under construction in the back of beyond, by the dusty shores of a lake. Africans in red shirts, diminished to the size of flies, crawl on the dam-face on scaffolding. We go round the lake. It's a beautiful day. Someone is obliged to get out of the truck every mile or so and open and shut gates, and all day long we pass through this curious landscape.

As the sun is setting we come out onto a dust road that leads to Uitenhage. The cars that pass leave behind them a long wake of dust. Then we come upon this town built upon an outcrop of little hills: Uitenhage. We've come from Somerset East.

At the hotel we are booked in, some mail is waiting. In our room the furniture reaches to the ceiling; the floor shakes and there's a continuous roaring coming up from the bar directly below us. It must be pay-day. We have a shower, change, go down to dinner. We have Cape white wine – quite good. Some of the company go to a film afterwards. I try to read, but the roaring below is a distraction. It's like a waterfall.

Next day we set up our marionette stage in the town hall. Jay and I go for a walk. The streets are wide, the buildings solid-looking, there are many Cape Malays; they seem in an atmosphere of old and settled gentility – so it must be a pretty remote spot, this Uitenhage.

The road runs out of town in a descending curve. Coming up the hill are some Malays and their jaunting-cars with big wheels and outsize hoods, coming in with provisions; it's just like in the old colonial times here. We pass one of these, its white hood and white wheels, driven by an old man; he has a brown, wizened face, wears a white linen suit and carries a long stick which he waves over the mule's head. He salutes us – this is strange enough in itself. We return his salute; out walking just like in the olden days. He waves us on with his long whip.

II

We walk up to a plantation of orange trees to catch the evening sun. It's outside a dusty dorp – name forgotten. The ground is raked between the orange trees. We sit there smoking and admiring the view. We see a stately home far away between the orange trees. It's somewhere in the Cape. Then we hear this thudding noise: something is coming towards us. We get up in a hurry.

Forty yards off, going parallel to us, two ostriches go jinking by, ruffling their feathers, spurning the ground with their great prehistoric feet, their protuberant eyes staring straight ahead.

III

The coldness of nights on the Karoo. Up on the chill plateau lives an Afrikaans community, tight-fisted and suspicious. It's another small dorp. Coming in, we pass two white down-and-outs covered in dust, carbonized in appearance, old, gravely saluting each other on Piet Retieffstraat; voortrekker stragglers.

A depressing hotel at world's end. Swing doors on the bar like in the Wild West. The habitués look all the same – tough, ugly, weather-beaten Afrikaans farmers, poor farmers? Share-croppers? Stench from the bar and the bedrooms none too clean either. In the patio a lame, injured tortoise drags itself into the grass.

Outside, in the white glare, a line of khaki trousers belonging to Afrikaans police constables blows on a clothes-line. It's blowing all the time; the air shimmers. We have poor houses. Loading the stage at night, after midnight, it's freezing. Remote freezing night sky full of stars. Is this the *platteland* at last?

Loxton. It's a town; it exists. The wind buffeting the

trees, and gross bulldogs on the ground. A town of bull-dogs, surly brutes. A modern town hall – austere, Dutch Reformed.

Over the veranda of the hotel there's a mattress with a hole charred in the middle. The night before, a commercial traveller, far gone in drink, fell asleep with a lighted cigarette in his hand, and woke up with the bed on fire. The others encounter him in the bar, his home from home; blank stare and stout heart. A great imbiber of good old Oude Meester brandy, man. He invites the whole company, including the three charming girls, to be his guests at a *braaivleis* after the show. It'll be late, after midnight, for it takes more than an hour to bag the puppets, dismantle and pack the stage.

So, after midnight, his African 'boys' cook meat for the marionette company, with several fires burning on the veldt, and plenty to drink; this is the life, man. When the 'boys' have finished cooking the meat he dismisses them, 'Get going, you buggers!' The poor buggers turn and begin tramping away. It's a five-mile hike back to town. Only after an argument will he allow them to stay, take something to eat. Going back, they stand on the running-board of his car. Halfway back he stops, falls asleep over the wheel. The day has been too much for him.

At seven next morning we are leaving Loxton again. I look into his car; he's there, fast asleep and dead drunk in the back of the car; the windows closed and his face blackish purple, a dead cigarette between his fingers, which were stained to the knuckles with nicotine. Rembrandts. Broken and mutilated creatures, best rendered by their own debris.

IV

The warm outdoor baths of . . . (name forgotten) Berkley East? Skin of a dead lamb hung on barbed wire. (Where?) The baths are thrown open at night for the London

12

marionette company. Pool and grotto and changing-rooms constructed during the war by Italian POWs. It's mid-winter, chilly, but the water is warm, greenish and trans-lucent under the electric light. Jane Tyson submerged.

Approaching Fort Beaufort in the cool of the evening, we pass a line of young African bucks trotting by in the dust of the road, all stark naked, daubed with white lime from the crowns of their shaven heads to the toes of their thick, misshapen feet; some carrying sticks, some with burdensome erections: tattooed amakweta trotting by in the cool of the evening, their childhood behind them.

News: Apostolic Brother commits nuisance with Bantu girl in the bushes at Aliwal North, justly famous for its healing therapeutic springs. Caught in the act, he denied it all: 'I was singing hymns to myself and praying.' Hymenal. Not acquitted.

Dutch Reformed Church dominie (85) commits *crimen injuria* with nubile African girl (25) under a car in a garage in Berkley East. Not acquitted.

No one walks with impunity under palms.

The Institute for the Blind at Worcester. The blind children working the machines. At the matinée, the teach-ers tell them what's going on: '*Dit is 'n poppenspiel, kinders.*' Later, still as silent, dumb children sitting under the trees as it's getting dark, knitting, reading Braille.

V

Report on Touws River. A freckled young woman with brawny arms staring over a wall, looking for trouble. What trouble can one create in Touws River? She's carrying on with a stout, flushed fellow in a striped bushranger shirt who stands on the near side of the wall (our side), affecting indifference. She waves a carving-knife playfully at him. He has short-cropped fair hair; he stares off down the road, over the bridge, where Bantus are walking into town dressed in ochre-coloured blankets, carrying provisions on their heads.

After a while he climbs the wall, drops down the other side and suffers himself to be embraced. She stands behind him with her arms about his neck. He stares down the road at the approaching Bantus; a carving-knife waves before his eyes. 'Och, min, I kud drive it into yew! I ked cut yew!'

Valsh River and floods, vane and weathercock; intricate silhouettes in sheet metal. The thin shagged spire of the *kerk* rises over the hill.

Orange River: where the yellow weaver-birds build their cocoon nests in the branches of the willows that droop down over the water. Jay swimming naked across the river. The island.

A line of overburdened telegraph poles on the edge of the Kalahari Desert; every fourth or fifth pole weighed down with a nest as big as a haycock. The gregarious community birds.

VI

A *platteland* scene: at Bramfort, a small ill-lit dorp off the Golden Highway, in the neighbourhood of Bloemfontein. A rusty-bearded Ancient of Days sitting on the hotel step staring down at his hands and grimacing. Somewhere in the hotel women are imitating the high squealing of pigs. High-pitched shrieks of drunken laughter. Over the darkened houses, the lightning! Airlessness before a storm.

Deluges of rain. When it stops I go for a walk. Guitar music from some shacks in a field below the road. Africans coming down the hill from a location, out of sight. 'Do I know Jo'burg? I'll say I know Jo'burg!' African pride in the big city: the Big Time. 'Have you a drink for us, boss?'

I go back to the hotel for dinner. Two outsize waiters, 'coloureds', overblown, like Mack Sennett villains, soft on their feet. Sucking pig on the menu; dinner for 5s. 6d.

After dinner a thin lady carrying a Dutch Airlines grip accosts me in the hall: 'Are you by any chance a Roman Catholic priest?'

No, do I look like one? (scarcely) . . . have I a dog-collar?

'Ah but sometimes they go without!' (This with a wistful look.)

Outside it's pitch dark. No street lighting in Bramfort. I am tired of being in Bramfort.

Report: in an up-country high school with a roll-call of seventy girls (fourteen to eighteen years), five are pregnant. No one walks with impunity under palms.

A funeral on the coast. A small new Roman Catholic cemetery, the pall-bearers myopic old gentlemen, the undertaker a thin tall chap with pointed shoes, grey sponge-bag trousers and a frock-coat, who goes like a dancer on his toes, his hands out from his sides, leading the cortège by a roundabout route to the graveside. A box of rose petals handed out to the mourners. An inscription on stone.

VII

An eccentric couple on the coast: the Halishams. Madame Conny Halisham and Rodney, a retired bank manager, a sort of vague backdrop to the heavy drama. His wife, Conny, a famous singer in her day. She has a Jewish lover – a Chopin artiste, a remittance man, American. Rosenbloom. He toured the colleges giving concerts. He came to the Halishams' house, was invited to stay nine weeks, but caught a cold and stayed twenty-five years. His dentures not properly in, pop eyes, 'boozed madly'. Madame Conny Halisham used to model in the nude on a stinkwood table while the lover, Rosenbloom, sketched her. Continually reproaching him: 'You don't love me anymore. My body has deteriorated' (she is over sixty). He is getting on in years himself. She comes naked to answer the doorbell. The house is called 'As You Like It'. Coastal eccentricities.

The husband wears bloomers with a slit cut for the fly; pink celanese underwear. They have adjoining rooms in the hotel. He puts his feminine underwear in the wife's wash-basket; the maid holds it up and inquires whether she can mend the hole. On the beach the husband sits in a pool, Madame Conny fumbles about, trying to get one last stand; never successful. Continuous reproaches.

They keep pug dogs – these are 'all over the furniture'. A bitch confined in the middle of the night. The husband phones his friend Dr Donnolly. 'I am not a vet, Halisham.' 'The poor dog is in great distress' (panting himself like a Pekinese). 'Prepare yourself for tragic news, man.' Calling the doctor 'Dr Jesus' when in favour, 'Dr Shit' when out of favour.

Calling, calling.

VIII

Coming from the Transkei, the vegetation changes all along the road, and by the time we reach the coast at Natal we have left the winter behind and it's summer again. Jay in the hospital at Pietermaritzburg being operated on for appendicitis.

The golf course at Pietermaritzburg. The Indian pro. Subtropical flowers. The warm wind off the estuary and spongy grass underfoot.

May 2nd–30th, 1957. Phoenix Hotel, Moltino, Cape Province. This Foreign Legion outpost reminds me of Aran. The same famished hens, weary mistrustful peasants, the same high winds.

We toured the West Karoo for a dull month and are now creeping up the east coast towards Durban.

July 1st, 1957. Marine Hotel, Port Shepstone, Natal. Here we are in Natal at last. A sort of third-rate Garden of Eden.

Outside this room . . . paw-paw trees, orange and banana, wild palms. I can see the sea. Dull grey day.

We passed through the Transkei and East Griqualand on the way here. Astounding lands. Native Reserve Territory.

Our Afrikaans driver, Brink by name and brink by nature, has stomach ulcers but refuses to either diet or stop drinking. He was also instrumental in getting old Joseph the African 'boy' sacked, and has added that pay onto his own. Brandy drinker. His eyes are bloodshot.

To date we have performed in just under a hundred towns, one more or less like the other. A sky soggy as pasture is releasing rain. The sea disturbed, the palms waving, remote cars passing on the road to Margate, where we play tomorrow. Warner Beach next Friday, and then no more touring until 20th. It will be a relief to finish.

September 2nd, 1957. Dixon's Hotel, Mafeking, Transvaal. In the past fortnight we have been as far north as Louis Trichardt, which is almost into Southern Rhodesia; as far east as Nelspruit, which is almost into Portuguese East Africa; and now as far west as Mafeking, the old siege town, which is within shouting, and shooting, distance of Bechuanaland.

Today is a public holiday. Settlers' Day. But not for this caravan. Jay is down with Asiatic flu and appears to be dying. In one way or another we are all suffering from travel fatigue.

Dixon's Hotel was the GHQ in the famous siege. The tattered original flag is preserved behind glass in the town hall where we are to perform with puppets today. A dreary monument to the fallen stands in front, hard by the waterworks. The plaque says: To the Memory of the Members of the Cape Boy Contingent . . . the Native Finco Contingent . . . the Black Watch . . . & the many Hundreds of Coloured and Native Non-Combatants who died by shot, shell and starvation, in Memoriam. Siege. King's Royal Rifles. And a roll-call of enlisted men who succumbed of wounds and diseases.

17

Today in the town hall, native servants, ill-paid and dejected, move about dusting the seats in a dream.

Outside, it's hot in the sun. Spring begins here.

Death is a silent picture, a dream of the eye; such vanishing shapes as the mirage shows.

Everywhere the peaceful face making way for the violent face. The actual terrain, too, violent. Violent colour, violent, combative contrasts, violent forms.

By November 30th we will have performed in 192 towns, and given over 400 performances ... prior to Rhodesia.

Ansonia Hotel: the most pleasant of the entire tour – and we must have stayed in over 200 hotels. The tall good-looking receptionist in the sack dress with the haughty eye (just you try). A mock-Tudor lounge in the grounds; an annexe with organ music. One Saturday night the resident organist dropped dead at the keyboard.

In the hotel grounds a lady guest in a red cardigan sits under the tall palm trees with a birdcage on her lap and stares at the canary. Stone tables like sundials are arranged informally; we sit there at peace, drinking gin. We are refitting and rehearsing a new programme in Natal University while the students are away. In the back of the auditorium I find two battered bowler hats, a tree with a single green leaf and some programmes – stage props for a past production of *Godot*.

The Notebooks of Malte Laurids Brigge in a second-hand bookshop, and a breast-feeding mother inquiring for the latest van der Post. The bookshop lady is very polite. 'And how is the milk, Mrs So-and-so?' 'Oh eets jest grained, thenks.' She improves the quality and quantity by eating lots of peanuts and drinking lots of milk. Imbecile cheerfulness of young parents.

A dead donkey on the roadside outside Durban; it's stiffened feet in the air, dried blood about the mouth and anus. Guarded by another Neddy, standing there dejected with downcast head. Fast-moving traffic into an industrial town.

Small coloured flags, put there by Indians to ward off evil spirits, in the high mango trees on the road into Durban.

Zululand, *op!*

IX

A deserted beach that goes on and on. Shores of light. A dolphin-torn, gong-tormented sea. Free of the others at last we spend most of the day sunbathing and swimming a mile or so down the beach: Adam and Eve in the white dunes. An Easter break at Keurbooms Rivier. Chalets. The sandy path to the sea. Brink, our Afrikaans driver, is shacked up with the local post-mistress's assistant and seldom appears.

One day in a clearing I come upon some Africans breaking in a horse. A stallion. It rears up, rolling a fearful reddened eye. A little brown man strikes fearlessly at its head.

Wide-open eyes; bursting lungs.

X

Travelling from Maseru to Ladysmith in the Orange Free State, we come to the customs shed on the Basutoland border early in the morning – five or six o'clock – and all in a bad humour, cooped up together too long, suffocating with heat and dust inside the National Theatre bus, which keeps breaking down every second day or so. This ochre earth. About to re-enter British territory, or a Protectorate, with no flag flying from the mast.

Two African customs men in khaki uniforms; one sitting on a chair outside the post having his hair clipped, his dusty tufts. Flash of the scissors. The Union Jack wrapped about his neck.

These are figures cut loose from a frieze; what you see of

them – the little you can see of them – it's only a very small part of their existence; their existence in my eyes. It's nothing. These are unknowable shapes.

Under the feet of the oxen in a field or roosting in the low trees by the river, showing up as blobs of white against the dark masses of the leaves – tick-birds, the sacred white ibis; venerated in holy India, but not here.

The Rhodesias

Over Beit Bridge one breathes a different air: different and cheaper brands of cigarettes and spirits for sale beyond the Limpopo. Bulawayo, Fort Victoria, Gwelo, Umtali, Salisbury, Blantyre, Kariba Dam, Livingstone, Victoria, Lusaka, Broken Hill, Ndola, the Copperbelt – all lie ahead of us. In Northern and Southern Rhodesia, and in Nyasaland, we will stay, whenever possible, in private houses, to defray hotel expenses, which are double that of the Union.

Here in Southern Rhodesia the settlers speak – not without ingenuousness – of the 'Yew Kai', the good old Yew Kai, or United Kingdom, by which they mean 'home'. The Afrikaans settlers, on the other hand, do not speak of Holland as home, far from it.

Many of the Africans here suffer from bilharzia and are hardly fit to assist in unloading and then loading again late at night. They seem to have no energy, let alone gaiety. Bilharzia – it's a form of sleeping sickness; those who suffer from it are listless, rather emaciated, seldom smile, and urinate blood.

February 23rd, 1958. Umtali, Southern Rhodesia. My teeth pain me, and the Rhodesian tour begins in floods of diarrhoea and torrents of rain. One listens under mosquito netting to the sting song of the skeeters. The nights are alive and warm, teeming with insects.

So. Delays by day at flooded rivers; sometimes a whole day goes by waiting for rivers to subside, and the schedule, in a few cases, goes awry. We go on. Wright drives us hard.

It's raining in Bulawayo. The rainy season drags on here, the rivers come down in flood, swamping the low-level bridges. It's a pleasant place with fancy homes set back among trees and ground-rents are high. Hillside, Bulawayo, an oasis. The McNairs.

Cigarettes are cheap. We buy boxes of fifty at a time. Scotch 26s. a bottle. We are X-rayed, injected against cholera, smallpox and yellow fever. The girls may go into bars.

The low skyline and wide streets, oxen carts going through brown rainwater. A copy of *A Portrait of the Artist as a Young Man* in Christian Vigne's bookshop. Wide tree-lined streets of Bulawayo, skyscrapers of Salisbury, and Africans so limp with bilharzia they can hardly lift a load.

The suffocating heat of Wankie. Tintinnabulation of diamond-doves – cracking heat itself. Baboons in the baobab tree outside the Baobab Hotel. Its air-cooled bar.

The native compound where we played on a cement floor. Dire warnings posted up against venereal disease behind us. The ruined homes in the crudely illustrated warnings: Africans, Africans, beware of the pox!

Victoria Falls. We drive from Wankie after only a few hours' sleep. Walking in the rain forest. Livingstone. African helpers weak with bilharzia.

Kariba. An Ethiopian-born Italian who can speak English acts as translator. An Italian town built on African hills. The Italian workers send seventy per cent of their wages home, fraternize with African girls. Kariba Dam at night; the partly completed dam walls. The blondins, operated from towers, weigh fifteen tons, stand ten feet high and cost £100 an hour to operate. When filled, the reservoir will be sixteen or seventeen thousand feet deep and about as wide as the Caribbean. No apartheid here. Lion tracks in the fresh cement of the landing-strip.

Salisbury Hotel. A grey, wispy painting in the lounge, a

view of Victoria Falls – made of porridge and pubic hair? Hatfield. Drive-in cinemas vast as Roman amphitheatres. The sky at night about Salisbury.

Curiosities: a battlemented 'Scottish' castle, turreted, built of stone, a private lake, a swimming pool among the rocks – a Union Jack flying over the castle. Owned by a cattle baron, now in his sixties, with incipient jigs. He drinks heavily; it's given him his dark mottled complexion, his red, saltpetred cheeks, his gout, shaking hands; yet he's a good host, if he cares to remember you. He started out 'banging sleepers' on the railway; look at him now. He buys and sells cattle to the Africans. We watch him setting out on another auctioneering expedition, dressed in a white linen suit, pith helmet, a monocle, riding boots, ultra pukka. His memsahib looking like nothing on earth. A luxury station wagon is loaded up with provisions for the trip by a line of faithful black family retainers. Bwana come; bwana go; bwana pretty damn rich. A kind of Gatsby.

Some of the company stayed in the castle. We had dinner there when he was gone. It came up through the service hatch. He has a good cook, a cellar. The dining-room hangs out over the ravine with a view of the lake. English hunting prints hang on the walls; a copy of *À rebours* (probably a mistake) among his nondescript books. In the split-level lounge – a beautiful long room – a Japanese officer's sword hangs in its scabbard on the wall.

We go to a fancy-dress party at Salisbury. The long avenue through Fortune's Gate; the tenants' houses on the estate are mansions. The architect's wife. Yashmak. Wonderful eyes. She wouldn't take it off. A double-barrel name, English; the cattle baron, safely returned, buying rounds of Scotch. Drinking gimlets in the air-conditioned bar; African waiters in scarlet tunics.

Tea-plantations of Rhodesia; acres and acres of tea-bearing bushes. The rich Italian brothers. The ballroom in their mansion set aside for the marionette show. Avarice and prosperity beyond the Limpopo. The dead dog run

22

over outside the hotel at Umtali; the row of gaping Indian children. The well-dressed crowd at the hotel door; an elderly lady takes it upon herself to examine the corpse, the bloodied roadway, dog's brains. The Indian children, darkly beautiful, gape at her.

A generous tobacco farmer offers Jay a sixteen-foot python skin, a twelve-inch hole blown in its head, as a memento, for a handbag or a pair of shoes; she refuses.

The closed-in Copperbelt. A whiff here of something ill; the neurosis of white Africa living and working close to its wealth. Theatres and swimming pools for this hard-drinking and soured community.

Lusaka; dinner with the abominable Pulsford. The spirit's features stiffen into the social grin.

Mufilura, Northern Rhodesia. A copper mine. Italian miners stuffing themselves with canteen food and drinking Chianti, their fat posteriors bulging over the chairs; in the midst of adversity I am preserved.

Kitwe. Night on the road; the embankment of slag from the blast furnaces. Tippers coming by rail all night long, one every twelve minutes. The molten slag pouring down into the darkness; two figures (African or white?) outlined by the glare. Poured once, in error, on an African worker.

Blantyre, Zomba, Tet. Portuguese imported white wine in Tet. Arab dhows tacking across the fast-flowing Zambezi. Arrival in the evening. The ill-natured monkey chained to its perch in the yard; yet a feeling of Europe here.

One last image: Dedza valley in Nyasaland. The long straight dust road through the pine forest. Grey, granite highlands, and a damp mist coming down over the hills. Relief at last from the perpetual heat and sweating. Drinking tinned Watney's and Scotch. A green secluded valley.

From the Cape to Kitwe, via Basutoland, Nyasaland, Natal, Southern and Northern Rhodesia, how many thousands of miles, how many towns, in more than two years' work for the John Wright Marionette Co. of London?

The tour ends somewhere near Salisbury. Exhausted, tired of the company, we are going back to Johannesburg.

PART TWO

'Are you ready, Friday?' said I. 'Yes,' says he. 'Let fly,
then,' says I, 'in the name of God!' and with that I
fired again among the amazed wretches, and so did
Friday; and as our pieces were now loaded with what
I called swanshot, or small pistol bullets, we found
only two to drop, but so many were wounded, that
they ran about yelling and screaming like mad
creatures, all bloody, and most of them miserably
wounded . . .

'Now, Friday,' says I, laying down the discharged
pieces, and taking up the musket which was yet
loaden, 'follow me'; which he did with a great deal of
courage; upon which I rushed out of the wood . . .

> Daniel Defoe, *The Life and Adventures of*
> *Robinson Crusoe*

The City

I   66 Loveday Street

Beginning again, jobless. We have managed to put by £200 from the tour. Jay in the Eastern Province with her parents.

Walking in Joubert Park. Johannesburg, where the trams go by, clanging by up the hill into cosmopolitan Hillbrow. I am staying in the Shotley Hotel near by, facing the park.

Tall Lombardy poplars agitated by the wind, tall blocks of flats in Hillbrow out of which come African nannies in white and blue uniforms and their charges, pampered Jewish children who have the run of this pleasure-ground. In the dining-room I share a table with three elderly women. Miss Duller. Personal napkin rings and turkey every Friday. On Fridays I invest in a tin of Benson and Hedges.

An old wheezing female guest in the hotel foyer: 'I'm beginning to feel better, more like a human being, now that the summer's coming in.'

Nights are very cold and I have difficulty getting to sleep. Obliged to invest in an electric fire. Chill mornings. Temporary employment at Constantia Bookshop in Loveday Street. Mevrouw van Overbeeke (who owns the place) and Juffrouw Moon (in the order and dispatch department) are Dutch; Herr Hodge Melville and Herr Weltsch are German – the latter Jewish. Herr Weltsch formerly worked on the *Berliner Tageblatt*; he watched the Reichstag fire burning. A small, stooped man with pebble spectacles, a hypochondriac, married four times, allergic to snakes. He works

27

overtime every evening, needlessly, spends the weekends in bed, all the windows of the flat bolted. His fourth wife, Rachel, groans at parties: '*Weltschian klein*, time to go home. Time to come home, *Weltschian klein*!'

I am to take over Juffrouw Moon's job when she is on holiday. The foreign community of Johannesburg subscribe to continental magazines: *Epoca, Quick, Tempo, Marie Claire, Domenica del Corriere*. Never err where Kligger and Gluck are concerned, Juffrouw Moon counsels me. (Are they miners, rich, irascible, set in their ways, who must not be crossed?) *Poètes d'aujourd'hui; Morceaux choisis*.

Herr Weltsch on the telephone: 'Miss Moore? [interrogatory] . . . Miss Moore! [ingratiatingly]. Ah Miss Moore [triumphantly] . . . I just laid my hand today on that book on Persian carpets.'

I just laid my hand. *Trapping Methods for Bird Ringers. Constipation and Our Civilization (With Suggestions for Home Treatment)*. Pauper beginnings; Monday mornings in winter, stale air and customers farting.

II   47 Kapteijnstraat

I move again – to austere lodgings at 47 Kapteijnstraat, a small toy house presided over by a very fat and asthmatic Afrikaans woman, Mrs Swannepoel. It's like a toy house with her in it; she fills it to overflowing. Obese and indolent, she spends most of her day in bed. The housework is done by a bony and elongated Zulu *hexendoktor*; his expression is severe, mask-like, and he has a bitter smell; he cleans and dusts the rooms and stairs, very louring – a forbidding manner. Mrs S., looking out from behind the screen, rubicund, newspapers scattered all over her bed. All well upstairs? Yes, all well. And your wife? Yes, coming any day now.

Behind, on the walls, framed pictures of generations of cats and dogs.

Beginning again.

III   My colleagues

Such strange colleagues. Hodge Melville is fair-haired, anaemic-looking, a placid, abstracted young gentleman; as a child when the war ended, he walked unlikely distances in Germany searching for his parents. Did he ever find them? He is in the accountancy section under Herr Weltsch.

A *tsotsi* pulled a gun on him in broad daylight, down at the African bus terminus, and demanded money. Hodge Melville, his thoughts miles away, brushed past him.

IV   Sjambok

Disquieting image: the maddened young policeman. The African girl flying for her life. She races down the path into darkness – the young constable, his belt loose, in hot pursuit. A passing car goes grinding up the hill towards the water-tower. From another, parked outside a block of flats, a squat young man emerges, a sjambok in one hand, his lip curling – retribution itself. No one sees; no one stops or cares, it's late, darkness covers all.

V   Street fight

One evening, driving along Jeppe Street, we witnessed the end of a knife-fight in one of the car parks there – about as public a place for it as, say, Cambridge Circus. Two African women were fighting. One was bleeding heavily, her dress hanging in flitters about her hips. They had one weapon between them – a bread-knife. A circle of men surrounded them, making no effort to interfere. The one who was cut was screeching, naked from the hips up. A long line of cars had stopped before the traffic lights.

They came to grips again, the injured one wailing at the top of her voice; in the scuffle she wraps her legs around the other and hauls away at her hair. They fall, the knife dropping from the other's grasp. The injured one takes it and jumps free. It seems likely now that murder will be done. The men seem to think so too. As she runs at the other, one of them takes her from behind; he pins her arms to her side. She thrashes about, screeching, her breasts wobbling and bloody.

Her opponent makes off, flying over by the pedestrian crossing and away like the wind down one of the intersecting streets leading to Bree Street.

The injured one frees herself and follows, barefooted, half naked, bleeding profusely, running right through the traffic which has begun to move again. She chases the other, brandishing her bread-knife, screeching. Her thin shoulder-blades move in and out; she is brown and dusty with a narrow compelling head, her ears pierced for small brass earrings.

Brown and windowless, as though gutted by fire, battered 'non-European' trams are rounding the corner by Florian's Restaurant, entering cosmopolitan Hillbrow.

VI   Zoological notes

In the Johannesburg Zoo a dishevelled giant condor on its perch shakes its soaked feathers, an ugly blue vein throbbing on its bare skull. It thrusts its scrawny neck out, watches through sluggish blood-filled eyes the jackdaws that come and go out of its cage.

An outing of female white patients from a mental institute sitting on the grass near the exit, staring about them with freak stares. Their movements are stiff, semi-paralysed.

The African men in smart city hats, sharp suits and well-polished black shoes, laughing at the shameless baboons; slapping themselves, mimicking the animals. A pit of excrement, a laughing face.

Outside the zoo, sprinting towards us in the bright sun,

a white man comes running with his topcoat thrown open, a wide-awake hat on the back of his head, glaring up at the sky. High-stepping, he holds to his breast a framed picture of the Sacred Heart. And so round the corner and out of sight.

Autumn colours, dry sunshine of the high Rand.

VII   Munts

Cheating. The African garage attendant at Yeoville was cheated of ten shillings by two of the *Herrenvolk* who drove up for gasoline in a battered, mud-caked Dodge, up from the *platteland*. They swore they'd given the bleddy Kaffir man a half note, man. But they didn't wait when he went for the owner; drove off, cursing us and him.

VIII   Beggary and destitution

An armless African beggar has a pitch by the lamp standard at a corner near Jeppe Street post office. His charity box is often empty. I have often wondered how he eats, since his arms are only stumps six inches long.

One day I saw an African boy bring him a double-decker sandwich from the Dutch delicatessen opposite the Monte Carlo Bio. The armless one watched me, rolling his eyes, the cornea brown and discoloured; the sandwich pressed up against his cheek, held in place by thrusting his shoulder up, and so brought it to his mouth in this manner. He gives me a haggard look for interrupting him at feeding time. Void heart, go on.

IX   Street scenes

(a) Africans at lunch-break, squatting on their haunches, their hands hanging, ape-like, loose at the wrists, over their knees, biding their time. They crouch there on spatulate feet, dusty and eroded in appearance, dressed in tatters: Java Man of 500,000 years ago. Crouching in Plein Street, in Market Street, Marshall Square, watching the action, the passers-by; sitting on the kerbside along Kruis Street playing cards or a rudimentary kind of draughts, using bottle caps, drinking tea from tin cans and stirring it with a wire clothes-hanger. A well-dressed one studying a textbook on criminal law. When I question him he does not reply, looking up at me, but not deferential, rightly suspicious of Special Branch spies and informers.

(b) Another day outside the Supreme Court of Justice, during the second year of the interminable Treason Trial, an enigmatic figure stood near the side doors by the German cannons captured by South African troops in German South-west Africa. An elderly white eccentric dressed in a grey suit, with plus-fours, a workman's blue denim shirt, a black beret puffed up on his head, an eye-guard covering one eye; smoking a briar pipe and gazing about him in a frank open way, observing the Africans without apparent animosity. He had a rather flushed face, and one leg was up on the spoke-wheels of a cannon; surrounded by black tutelary spirits waiting there at the side door without much hope, in the rags and tatters of extreme poverty. One in a loose white shirt stands on crutches, his shoulders hunched up level with his ears so that he appears to be sprouting wings.

(c) Library Square: a hot griddle in summer. Haunt of disreputable white drunks. They assemble here, brandy drinkers and sherry drinkers, on seats reserved for 'Europeans Only'. *Blankes, nie-blankes.* In the winter they hitch-hike to the Natal coast, these men and women with

32

discoloured faces, who act as contacts between the Africans and the bottle-stores.

A Relation of Some Yeares' Travaile into Afrique by Sir Thomas Herbert (1634) in the City Library. The troglodytes. In place of circumcision, the men pull away 'one ftone, fearing to beget too many children'. The women give their children suck as they hang at their backs, 'the vberous dugge ftretched ouer their fhoulder'. Mendelssohn had a copy, formerly the property of Jonathan Swift. Genesis of Gulliver?

In the hot griddle of the square, confronted by the blackened faces of the drunkards, male and female, his gloomy view of mankind does not seem too extreme.

X   A stabbing

The freelance commercial artist. His troubles that we are now a party to. His wife divorced him and now has custody of the two young children. He is convinced it's a frame-up with the father-in-law (a lawyer) behind it; so stabs him in the back and ends up under observation (the father-in-law trying to have him certified, trying to get possession of his car) in an institute. The lawyer, the ruthless one, recovers. His victim moves to another flat; he works late at night (it's a kind of neurosis with him). In one of the flats below, facing his flat, another light burns late. The commercial artist goes onto the balcony for a breath of fresh air at 4 a.m. Another man is standing on the balcony opposite, staring across. The father-in-law again!

The divorced wife re-marries (a Jew); the victimized one takes the children every second Sunday. Sometimes this doesn't work out. The father-in-law again. The son-in-law by accident meets him, and is knocked senseless on the path. His opponent is a champion middle-weight boxer.

Next the son-in-law is in prison for brandishing a revolver before the ex-wife and the husband; the husband runs from the room. The ex-husband very theatrically threatens to kill himself. The ex-wife, protecting the frightened children, phones for the police. He shows her that the revolver is not loaded, then drops it in the tank of his car. The police come; he meets them empty-handed, all innocence. They find the revolver; he is thrown into prison.

His background: the eldest in a Dublin Catholic family of nine. The father at first indifferent to him, then becomes attached to him. They quarrel 'because their characters are so alike'. He emigrates to South Africa.

Seven years pass. He is travelling from Durban to Johannesburg at night; travelling at about seventy he runs over a horse asleep on the road. The front of the car is smashed, and the horse in a bad way. He has a small pistol, and fires three times into its head. The bullets bounce off: he's hitting bone. He puts the gun at an angle to the animal's ear and this time kills it.

He reached Johannesburg. That night he has a dream. In the dream he sees his father, now grown old and frail, going down the steep hill from Hillbrow. At the bottom, where the gradient is even steeper, the old man is tottering, almost running. The son follows him, crying out to him to be careful. He sees his old father before him in a dressing-gown tumbling over and striking his head a fatal wallop. The son knows he's done for; he wakes up covered in sweat.

A couple of days pass, then a telegram arrives, sent from Dublin and forwarded from Durban. It tells him what he already knows: the father died on the same day and at the same hour as the dream. (The son hasn't been home in twenty years; he had the dream thirteen years ago.)

XI   Big Mick

His preposterous Ulster friend Big Mick is in engineering; a muscular brute who suffers apparently from softening of the brain: he repeats his yarns over and over again, in the same room, to the same company. The wife, something on

34

the lines of Molly Bloom, florid, dressed to kill, her overflowing bust strapped in with difficulty, her wobbly rump, satin slippers – rather eccentric get-up. A stuffy flat in which one suffocates. Parties of unimaginable boredom. The grimaces of Big Mick waiting to be 'candidly' snapped lolling in his armchair, holding onto his dentures. The armchairs all have chintz borders and seem to be wading across the carpet. He once filed a story for *Time* magazine. He told us so himself, twenty times.

XII   Murder in Hillbrow

The impassive witness. Queers quarrelling; one shoots the other three times in the chest and makes his escape down the back stairs. A description of the dying man – shot thrice, he crawls along the ground outside a first-floor flat, blood oozing through the back of his shirt, moving his legs slowly sideways, his fingers in the cracks of the ground; he seems to be 'fornicating with the cracks'. Outside Ruth Levy's place. A witness hears the murderer escaping down the stairs.

November 1958. Johannesburg. In this city, which claims the highest suicide rate next to West Berlin, forty a week died from unnatural causes. One double-locks at night with a deadlock and lies awake listening to the howling of the watch-dogs. City of watch-dogs.

XIII

Simmonds Street, Marshall Street, Hollard Street, Syfret's Trust (Johannesburg Stock and Share Brokerage), the Chamber of Mines, Marshall Square. The uncertainty of beginning. Thin high cirrus masking the sun, but soon it's blazing forth again; blue skies and warm air of the high Rand, this marvellous winter climate. Nu-Nite Nitewear, morning haze. Kahn's for pianos. Everything lightens and tightens. The Republic is on its way. *Killer Ape* showing at the Bio-Café in Rissik Street. The tough ones lounging outside. Stench of popcorn and Jeyes fluid. Bawling of the vocalist, electrified. Black Sash ladies outside the town hall. A handful for the front. *Wedding in Springtime* at the Colosseum. Princess Margaret's wedding. *Irma la Douce* at the Brooke Theatre. One hundred and eleventh performance.

One grows weary of the long sameness of the days here. The only variety offered is the tropical storms which recur punctually at five every evening; but even of these one grows weary.

The roads, the commercial travellers, the quacks.

Dr Rex Ferris, specialist in *natuur-genesing . . . asma . . . swak longe . . . breuk . . . stinkasem mangels . . . katar . . . hardlywigheid . . . swak van du bloed . . . swak hart . . . hare watuitval . . . abgesakte maag . . . slegtesukalasie . . . blindedermontsteking . . .*

XIV

An African burglar, small and sceptical, sitting on a bed, holding up a mother and twenty-year-old daughter at gunpoint. Putting them through it. 'You tell me what white woman in Jo'burg hasn't got a gun and jewels. Go on, you tell me.' He locks them in the wardrobe, threatens to shoot them through the door, and so makes his escape, empty-handed. Then or later armed robbery carried the death penalty, for Africans.

XV   Marshall Square

I have on a few occasions noticed an elderly white woman of reduced circumstances standing at one of the corners of the square with an open suitcase in front of her on the pavement. She is trying to peddle homemade dolls, wretched objects priced at 5s. each. Nobody stops or looks at them; I have never seen anyone buy from her. She doesn't seem to mind. A patient bloodless face and unseeing eyes, thinking of something else, wishing she were somewhere else. Remnants of former respectability apparent. She wears the cast-off jacket of a man's blue suit, a hobble skirt, dark blue, lower at the front than at the back; on her head a bowl-shaped black raffia hat with a bull hatpin thrust through the crown, a scarf wound about the raffia. Tram-conductors pass her, those hard-faced young men going off duty, caps on the backs of their heads and their uniform jackets open. No one buys from her.

XVI   Dream of the snake and the African

Looking through the kitchen into Isipingo Street. A group of Africans surround something on the road. It's a snake. One of them puts his boot down on its neck; the snake coils itself about his leg, trying to spit its venom. Unable to stamp directly on its head, he stumbles, and struggles with the snake. They come nearer. I am terrified that the snake will fall on Jay, then five or six months pregnant.

The snake, still coiled about the boot, now appears outside the window (we are on the third or top floor in Mount Willmar). It has a flat squashed head and looks rather pathetic. On the point of falling not on Jay but on me it murmurs, 'I'm done for . . . have pity.'

The snakes of terror hiss around your head, and indeed around mine the snakes of fear hiss even wilder.

The day before, Todd Matshikiza and his coloured wife came to lunch. His story of standing in a queue in front of a scandalized Afrikaner at the snake-pit in Port Elizabeth. Origin of the dream? A childless couple.

XVII Daydream

Heavy rain, a shattered window, a death here. The murdered man with one arm inside. His body hangs outside, rain falls on his white shirt. Something that cannot be altered. Grey ghosts; grey ghosts of human speech.

XVIII

March 23rd, 1959. A day of bright sun in Johannesburg, with autumn leaves everywhere. Die flowers away. Feeling almost of Germany. The ring-tailed lemurs in their cage in the zoo alarmed by stirrings in the cage of vultures. Complacent postures against the bars, their faces up to the sun. Ra. They dangle their delicate hands. Eating paw-paw rinds.

One night I drove with F. to Jan Smuts Airport to meet her husband, who was flying from Capetown. Harry Oppenheimer was the first up the ramp off the Capetown flight. A few words in the baggage-man's ear and he departs in his car; the rest of the passengers wait patiently for their baggage to come up the escalator belt. The Capetown passengers standing about in the waiting-hall on a freezing night.

On the way back, we saw that an African had been run over attempting to cross near a traffic robot. There was some shattered glass on the roadway and a small crowd about the injured man. Two in yellow crash helmets looking at him and not saying a word. The injured man soaked in blood; he lay half on the footpath and half on the road holding on for dear life, and made a weary gesture to us.

The jazz opera *King Kong* at Witwatersrand University, and Miriam Makeba doing bumps and grinds on the stage – an African Maria Vivo. A 'mixed' audience; unprecedented warmth of reception. This is a Jewish-African affair, and the first movement towards a true national theatre in South Africa. Stuttaford's non-European staff and the non-European staffs of Greatermans, O. K. Bazaars, Arnhold & Co., Earthmoving Contractors, the Chamber of Mines, Lipworth & Co., Joko Tea, and Adamczewski ('I am not one of your Communist friends!') — all wish *King Kong* every success.

XIX

I go to work by the number 11 bus into town, a 5d. ride, by Gundelfinger & Weinraub, the Ord Tie Factory, Kahn's Pianos, by the municipal tennis courts where a bored coach in flannels and a peaked cap is lobbing brown balls over the net to an uninspired novice. I see Sybil Joffe getting out of her sister's dented car at 8.20 in the morning of a fine sunny day outside J. Walter Thompson's agency. I go on to 66 Loveday Street. Morning after morning.

On the morning bus. The bottom of Jeppe. Butcher's boy (Bantu) cycling alongside the number 11. A deep butcher's basket with a severed bullock's head inside. Bristles about the mouth, the eyes as if gouged out with a red-hot poker; some fury of resignation about the flayed mouth: a skinned death's head.

Looking down into the bedroom of one of the bungalows adjacent to Mount Willmar one night, I saw a man kneeling in his shirt and trousers by a double bed — sole support of a white family of only modest means. His wife was sitting bolt upright by the wall, knitting, looking over at the husband every now and then. His eyes closed, he clasps his hands in sudden ardour, bowing his head humbly to the Almighty; Lord, Lord, have pity on such as I!

XX   Seance

Miss Kerk, rich, masculine-looking owner of cheese factory, a childless spinster, adopts three children – Elizabeth,
Noel and Jemma.

They grow up. Noel, 'a bit retarded', found employment
as an overseer on the roads. Elizabeth married; the husband
was a good-for-nothing who used to beat her. She had two
children by him. The husband beat her when she was
pregnant with her third. In the nursing home in her delirium
she was crying out, 'Oh don't hit me! Please don't him me on
the back!' She died in childbed and the baby with her.

When she was dying she extracted a promise from Miss
Kerk that she would look after the two children. The
husband was not allowed to have custody of them, so the
Child Welfare Association ruled.

Then the spirit medium Alec Harris came to Johannesburg, and Miss Kerk went to see him. At the seance he
successfully invoked the spirit of the dead wife. She mater-
ialized and went straight to Miss Kerk, took both her hands
and laid her cheek against Miss Kerk's, calling her 'Markie'
– her old pet name for her – thanking her for all she had
done and was still doing for her two children, and this with
great feeling.

The scene of pine, eucalyptus and peppergum at Observ-
atory, an accumulation of scents; the warm wind, dry
eucalyptus – a memory of Cavtat in Dalmatia. We have a
child now – a little boy; he cries out under the trees,
looking up from his pram.

On the hillside above the golf course the African Zionist
sects are singing and parading. It's a very energetic religion;
they march and counter-march among the trees near the
Benoni Road – the choral chanting of the bearded priests,
their deep voices raised in prayer, promises, objurgation.
The female supplicants answer with their thin banshee
wail. A canticle of psalms, a brotherhood of the bushes, the
voice of Africa at its lamentations. A multitude of insects

rise over the grass; it's evening time, the sun going down over the hill. The insects show up palely, agitated; the golfers are going home. The singing and the insects rise together, the golfers neither hearing the one nor seeing the other. We dream of living elsewhere . . . on St Helena, in the Seychelles. Endless life; endless choice.

The pedigree dogs in the ornate suburban haciendas along Urania Street bark at us, the same as at all intruders. The sun-drenched Daughters of Jerusalem are showing off their brown legs. The sprinklers revolve and revolve on the green lawns, widening their skirts of spray. Peaceful days in Johannesburg.

XXI   Morgan and McGaw

I am employed by a company that produces and markets short commercial advertising films. I am in the Scenario Department with my colleague de Wet.

We work in a shabby room on the sixth floor of a block of office buildings near the junction of Market and Kruis. My salary is adequate. In the office is a battered green filing cabinet, three desks (one connected to the General Manager's office by an intercom), an unshaded electric light that on winter days shines on bare and not particularly clean lemon-yellow walls. I am to spend a year here and save £800.

My immediate predecessor, I am told, was a drunkard. I never met him. I share the office with this weepy lunatic de Wet. Despite his Afrikaans name he affects a very pure BBC accent. He is on the phone throughout the day on matters of an excruciatingly private nature, weeping into the receiver, pleading for his happiness and whatever remains of his sanity to be returned to him – inanities of that nature. He is divorced, but has got himself engaged to another girl, though uncertain whether he should go through with it. He seems to enjoy sending her flowers.

41

However, it comes to nothing. This thin, pale, sickly-looking fellow is both very conceited, where women are concerned, and deeply neurotic, where his chances with them are concerned. He will leave a few months after my arrival.

His successor, McGaw, is hardly an improvement. McGaw has the identical BBC-announcer accent as de Wet, the identical fastidious intonation. Edinburgh-born, with a failed career in advertising behind him. He is portly and middle-aged, with stooped shoulders, a bad complexion and red-rimmed eyes. He has run to fat, has a great beaked nose, and is very nervous. A balding pate and an indecisive manner; wears spectacles, is gallant with the ladies; has an awkward flaccid deportment, rolling and pitching on uncertain feet, shoulders bowed and eyes to the ground. Not in his health. A *reformed* alcoholic. Market Street knows him.

He makes his job seem very difficult. He uses a top-heavy office Underwood, single spacing on yellow copy paper, correcting his scripts in pencil (second thoughts) and ball-point (third and fourth thoughts). He is not very good at his job and – what's more to the point – is far from adroit in his handling of the General Manager.

XXII   McGaw's tics

A hacking cough, developing into convulsions, chewing boiled sweets, visiting the WC twenty-five times a day, opening the window to read the time off Mosenthal's clock fifteen times a day, grinding his molars (another boiled sweet), restlessly shifting his position on the leather seat of his swivel chair, yawning, wiping his spectacles.

He lives in fear and dread of the buzzer going: a summons from the tyrannical General Manager to have his script subjected to severe scrutiny. Morgan the GM bullies and harries him whenever he can.

The buzzer goes; McGaw draws in his breath, swallows,

pushes down the button, says 'Yes, Mr Morgan.' Tyrant Morgan's acid voice says: 'McGaw – come in, will you?'

The squeaking of his swivel chair. It has a pin loose. Every fourth or fifth day, for light relief, it comes loose; McGaw then up-ends it and struggles with it on the floor. Then he has to go and wash his hands. De Wet is hardly ever in the office; McGaw is hardly ever out of the WC.

He perspires a lot, wipes his forehead constantly with Kleenex, yawns his head off, removing his heavy-rim spectacles to pluck at his albino eyelashes, yawns his prodigious watery yawn, and then stoops again over his scored and much-amended yellow script, already two days overdue. Would it do? . . . Would it ever do?

His nerves are on edge, and he cries out involuntarily when objects fall: the sudden smash of a saucer on the floor makes him start from his chair and cry out. Morgan continues to humiliate and harry him.

Mr Morgan is in the moviola room viewing a rough-cut and wishes to see Mr McGaw – the message comes through the private secretary. McGaw, with the memory of recent humiliations fresh in his mind, tacks from side to side down the detested corridor, his shoulders hunched, leering at the switchboard girl as he passes her open door; he holds in one hand sheets of yellow copy paper, added to and held together with clips, the whole typed in cramped single spacing and corrected with pen and pencil in his meticulous handwriting. Mr Morgan is in a wax in the moviola room.

XXIII Oslo

Mrs Gramm is a small, tubby lady, a Lithuanian Jewess, who works in another department, is sometimes available as a relief copy typist. Morgan is very particular about the appearance of scenarios and requires eight carbons. Mr Morgan, who knows everybody's business better than they do themselves, goes over the firm's books with Mrs Gramm. She does not care much for him. Her own husband was a quiet, dependable, studious man; they lived in Oslo. 'Quisling was my husband's riding-master,' she says with pride.

XXIV   The switchboard girl

The swaggering bum of the young switchboard girl. She has a good figure, wears very tight clothes. Her boyfriend is in the police. He's a patrol cop. Sometimes he calls – a hard-faced young Afrikaner in black leather leggings and cast-off SS uniform, blond hair cropped to the roots. He'll take no nonsense.

This girl is also bullied by tyrant Morgan. She weeps at the switchboard, her eyes swim behind thick lenses: 'Mr Morgan is no gentleman.'

XXV   McGaw again

Cold mornings on the sixth floor. The dry fug from the electric fire. In the resounding canyon of Kruis Street below us furniture is being dragged across the pavement and into new business premises, with a harsh grating noise like the roaring of lions. McGaw buffets open the window to stare at Mosenthal's clock and cold air comes in.

'I think I'm hep,' McGaw says, 'but I suppose the young people of today would consider me hopelessly square.' Another prodigious watery yawn engulfs him and his weak, red-rimmed eyes fill with tears; he wipes his eyes and nose with the corner of a Kleenex, pulling down his albino eyelashes. A boredom scarcely to be tolerated, witnessed or endured. McGaw's spongy feet, hacking cough, damp, damp hands.

O. Rubenstein, J. B. Pain, the Mental Health Society of the Witwatersrand, African Underwear Manufacturers – these names in turn are revealed to me. The lift stops – it's the ground floor; I get out with the others.

44

The streets, the evening light and heat, the bus-ride back to the flat. Liberation. Evenings on the balcony with Kensington mine-dumps in the distance. Drinking gin.

Going to work in the morning, walking along Kruis Street, I see a familiar figure in front, shambling along on his bear's feet, it's like locomotor ataxy – McGaw *en route* to further humiliations.

XXVI Eros

Sharply defined morning shadows in the intervening gardens separating our block of flats from another block across the way. Morning after morning the sun shines on a second-floor bedroom. Morning after morning a figure appears at the window to exercise naked after showering. Dark-haired and pale-skinned. The husband, a shadowy figure, moves in the background.

XXVII

Mornings in the Scenario Department when business is slack, or the free and easy times when the General Manager is away on business, driving hard bargains in Capetown, Durban, Port Elizabeth. McGaw relaxed.

'Chaps, do you realize that this time ten years ago I was burning archives in the gardens of the British Embassy at Liège? (peering at his desk calendar) . . . the 10th of May.'

My colleague who sucks – or rather *grinds* – boiled sweets throughout the day, for his nerves; visits the Gents fifteen to twenty times a day, for his incontinent bladder; who lives in dread of the General Manager.

'As I grow older I give less and less credence to the doctrine of Christian Science, though I believe their findings in psychoanalysis are sound enough.' Wisdom of McGaw.

I said: Yes, but didn't Roman Catholicism make this

discovery several centuries ago? 'Where, pray?' (raising a sceptical eyebrow). In the confessional, I say.

XXVIII   Sundowner Bar

The Sundowner Bar is in Jeppe Street next door to Pilgrim's Bookshop. It has an undistinguished façade, with two entrances. I go to the saloon bar during the ninety-minute lunch-break for purposes of meditation, and for the very good Hansa draught lager. It's chilled, and comes from Windhoek – a real German lager. It's a quiet bar, rather cramped, and might well serve as a stage model for the bar in *The Iceman Cometh*. The counter rather cramped too; the roof low, supported by imitation wooden pillars, with a fine cheating grain; a narrow place with real 'operatic' German barmen, stout and flushed, Hans and Richard – Chianti bottles on the wall and a fresco of Ludwig II's Schloss Linderhof. My eyes have gone up and down that lake, have hunted in that forest, oh hundreds of times.

The place is frequented by sallow-faced window-dressers, white drunks, riff-raff that this city glories in. Every day for more than a year I went there; it made Johannesburg tolerable for me. They served hot soup free on cold days.

The three regulars. Dr X, a Jew, qualified doctor, late of London, a hole-in-the-heart expert, very hard on the bottle. Some illegal practice perhaps? Abortion? He dresses in a dark morning suit with a waistcoat into the pockets of which he likes to put his fingers; a Derby hat pushed onto the back of his head; very waspish.

The second member of the trio is an Austrian count, very distinguished-looking, tall, well dressed; his habit of asking questions (sign of intelligence?). Before he war he worked for Skoda, the Czech munitions firm. He was in China when the war broke out, and came back via Mozambique; passing through the Union he was interned, and spent six years in a camp outside Johannesburg. Hans, the stout

barman from Westphalia, tells me all this. He was interned
with the count, and recalls the other's internee's pyjamas
with coronets stitched on the breast. He is less far gone in
drink than the other two; wears an Anthony Eden hat,
very tall, brown-faced man, a moustache, speaks English
with a German accent, a cutting edge. The type one sees
on the polo field. Always full of schemes for getting wealth
(gold?) out of the ground; schemes invariably crushed by
the doctor.

The third member of the party is a small, monkey-faced
Irishman out of Cahirciveen, his features dark and his
hands shaking from constant heavy brandy-drinking. Fitzy.
He left Ireland twenty years ago to seek his fortune in
Johannesburg. His hopeless, bleary eyes; telling me a story
concerning Wilde, of doubtful authenticity. Suspected
homo leanings, more out of hopelessness than nature.
Manages – fiddles? – the books for the taxi drivers on the
rank outside the bar. They are inseparable; sometimes
arriving by taxi, already a quarter shot; they never touch
solids for lunch, but put down six or seven double brandies.
Their range of interests is exceptional; inquiries put out by
the count, countered by the Jewish wiseacre, Fitzy plod-
ding after, a long way from Cahirciveen. Fugitives from
Nightwood.

The relief barman George is a shady character, not all in
it; member of the Deaf, Dumb and Blind Association of
South Africa, he has travelled the country from end to end,
as have I. Some curious beliefs. He hears voices. A furtive,
weasel-like, undependable man.

G. (furtively, behind his hand): I got the message again.
I: Yes?
G.: Jet Stream. It's a certainty. Put your money on now.
Nine to one. Jet Stream.
(He talks in spurts like this, like Mr Jingle.)
I: I never back horses.
G. (reassuringly): That's all right. Try Jet Stream.
I (wary): Who gave you the message?
George serves a customer a bottle of milk stout. Comes

up to me again, leaning forward, fixing me with his no-coloured eyes.

G. (with much conviction): I got it from another world, sir.

I: Which world?

G. (radiant): The one we all go to after this one, sir.

Long pause. George goes away; comes back.

I: But are the spirits of the other world interested in what goes on in this one? Are they interested in horses?

G. (very solemn, in measured tones): Sir, I assure you (leaning forward, giving me a blast up from his sour stomach), the spirits never lied to me. And they gave me great help all my life. Gawie (the Afrikaans owner of the Sundowner) put on £5 this morning and I put on £8. A certainty! Jet Stream.

Stout Hans from Westphalia glaring at him in flushed amazement.

XXIX

After a stormy scene McGaw is ignominiously sacked by tyrant Morgan — for general incompetence, slackness of application, incompatibility of temperament with the boss.

Some few weeks later I encounter him again, dressed in a white coat standing at a street corner, attempting to sell bibles; he expresses himself well satisfied with the open-air employment. Sinking, sinkingly.

XXX   Job reservation law

The African lift boys have been fired and their places taken by a set of incompetent Afrikaner harridans with stiff, henna'd hair-dos, conscripted from the lower stratas of SA society. They sit on the job, on small stools provided, talk as equals to their passengers, drink endless bottles of Coca-Cola, and have difficulty stopping the lift flush with whatever floor you want to get out on. They are of the same breed as the girls in mauve uniforms who work in the Film Room – as motley a crowd as you might hope to come across in all this remarkable subcontinent.

The Africans, decent, sober young men, have no alternative but to go; they leave without complaining, and without any alternative employment offered them.

J. B. Pain, the Mental Health Society of the Witwatersrand – a couple in the lift, mother and grown son, exchange a very wild look; the son's fixed stare, inimical glance of paranoia, the mother's hair standing on end, as if in a high wind; they go hand in hand down the corridor leading to the Mental Health Society of the Witwatersrand.

XXXI   Coalbrook

In January 1960 at Coalbrook Mine, 435 miners (six white) were entombed in a fall-in at 500 feet and buried alive, none were ever recovered.

In June there occurred the death of George Siwisa, leader of the banned Pan-African Congress, serving a three-year sentence for incitement, in Boksburg Jail. On the death certificate the cause of his death was made out as 'brain thrombosis'. He was buried next day by Cinderella Prison officials.

Three weeks later his daughter received a letter from the Bantu Commissioner's office in Pretoria addressed to 'the relatives of the late George Siwisa', and requesting that his clothes be removed.

Coming back hazily through the cut flowers of the Indian flower market behind the Supreme Court of Justice, I see a police van driving away from the door with the arms of African prisoners thrust through the bars at the back giving the Freedom Africa sign, and muffled cheering from inside the van.

49

XXXII   A weekend at Ferndale

It was two o'clock in the morning and we were alone in
the Mauthners' place at Ferndale. I woke up knowing it
was going to happen. A moment later I heard the smash of
the long window in the lounge being broken.

The bungalow, a German architect's home, had been
broken into two years previously and ransacked. They
didn't want that to happen again while they were away,
and so had asked us would we like to stay there for the
long weekend. Ferndale is some distance outside the city
on the Green Line bus route; a sparsely populated area
where well-to-do professional people have built houses. I
had been sitting all day reading Gibbon in the garden and
drinking cold Lion beer. After darkness fell the mosquitoes
came in great numbers (the fishmoths were already there
in the house – something to do with the water supply).
The rooms were very small and stuffy with not a breath of
air circulating. We couldn't open the windows once the
burglar alarm was set; neither could we sleep under the
mosquito netting.

After the window was smashed, we weren't sure that the
alarm would work. Jay pressed all the buttons. The alarm
started; it went on and on, wailing. Then silence. Not a
sound. I thought, 'They're all inside, waiting with their guns
out.' I waited ten minutes then unlocked the bedroom door,
went along the hall, opened the living-room door, switched
on the light. There was nobody there. I pulled back the
drapes. The long window was broken down its length.
Someone had tried to get in; there was the brick.

That bright sunny day, sitting in the garden drinking
Lion beer, looking at the rolling countryside, the blue
mountains where we'd gone climbing – the Magaliesburg
– with the vines turned yellow, syringa leaves, I thought
they would come back to finish what they'd started.

When it was dark again we sat there reading with the
drapes pulled back and the window broken so that a troop

of them could walk in, if they wanted to. We didn't set the
alarm, and spent a very uncomfortable night, waiting for
the blow on the back of the head, like the pigmy man in
the fairy tale. Next day the Mauthners came back.

XXXIII   Shabeen

There's one in Bellevue near the water-tower on a ridge
overlooking Bez Valley on one side and the area around
McKay Park and its Lombardy poplars, uniformed African
nannies and pampered over-fed Jewish children. It's close
to a municipal refuse dump that had been out of use for
some time, and overgrown with bluegum and peppergum
trees, with the rusted bodies of three or four cars that had
been left there to rot. On non-working days the Africans
went there, dressed in their best clothes, to drink Kaffir
beer – Basuto and Zulu, Amaxosas and Bantus in slick city
suits, white shirts, highly polished black shoes; their
women dressed in very full-gathered, slate-grey skirts, their
hair cut very short and wearing knitted woollen caps
brought into fashion by Miriam Makeba. All comporting
themselves with much dignity, hardly ever drunk, the
women staying in the background, ladling the thick beer
into billy-cans. The men squat on their heels or on the
rusted cars holding smoke-blacked tin cans in their pale-
palmed hands; sitting about there on the rocks, on the
lookout for the police (illegal for Africans to drink in white
areas, illegal to have shabeens), or in the shade of the
bluegum trees, calling out to their friends who pass by on
the road.

XXXIV   Gambling

There's a gambling school recess in Wyncliff Road. It's a
short cul-de-sac made up of blocks of expensive flats on

the left, terminating at the white palings before a mock-colonial Spanish edifice with front patio, geraniums, carriage lamps on the white wall. We often call on friends in Samedo there and have noticed this old battered Hudson always standing outside and the flat-boys sitting around it and in it. They are always hanging about there in their hours off duty; the car never seems to be driven anywhere.

It's one of the spoils of a big poker game.

The flat-boys are inveterate gamblers and play for high stakes. They put down a year's pay on a single game. The Hudson is always changing hands, but whoever wins it is afraid to drive it away. The gamblers who have owned it and lost it, sit on it or near it, touching it, waiting for their luck to change. So it remains where it is, weighed down by the weight of the gamblers. They wear the conventional flat-boy's uniform, the white cotton vest and knee-length pants with blue edgings that is the uniform of their bondage: a kind of light-opera convict garb. And barefooted.

Their life, however, is no light opera; at night we hear the raids, the boots on the fire escape, the police whistles, the crying and the bare feet running. We wait for gunshots. These raids are carried out in the early hours of the morning and are engineered by the ever-vigilant Special Branch, anxious to apprehend treasonable persons, Commies, black whores, run-of-the-mill infringers of the notorious Pass Laws.

Sitting on a dentist's chair on the sixteenth floor of an office building in the centre of Johannesburg, a view of flat roof-tops and washing blowing on lines, a flagpole with the Union Jack flying in the breeze, and on a distant mine-dump away towards Benoni, a white scarf of mine-dust blowing off the rim.

As and from tomorrow the British flag will be brought down and the new flag of the free Republic run up in its place. 'Out of the blue sky . . .' *Die Stem*. While I'm in the chair his ex-wife the novelist Nadine Gordimer phones to ask the dentist the meaning of being 'on the threshold of pain'. Gavronski tells her all about the threshold of pain.

XXXV   The air of the Rand

This quite wonderful and invigorating air, and the blue, blue skies of the high Rand. Portuguese East market gardeners. Thin high cirrus masking the sun briefly. A wild swan flying over the skyscrapers of Johannesburg; it must have mistaken it for a forest; no, it's a city – it turns back.

Martin de Kock in the Sundowner Bar. Folk wisdom. Baboons when shot cry like human babies. A remedy against their pilfering used by the farmers is to catch one, paint him white and let him loose again. Gregarious by nature, he runs for the herd. Terrified by his startling colour they flee from him; he can never catch up with them and dies of loneliness.

Karin the young lesbian has eyes of an ocelot. Looking down from the twentieth floor at City Heights at the suntanned beauty in the red bikini sunbathing beside the kidney-shaped swimming pool full of blue water, reflecting clouds passing high above City Heights, the sun blazing in mid-heaven.

Dapper brown-faced Portuguese East businessmen alighting from a train in the main rail terminal. One, very distinguished-looking, in a dark suit, spotless white shirt, carries a cane on the crown of which is pinned an orchid. If certain words were said to an old stick it would be covered in flowers and leaves and would take root again. *Kandogya-Upanishad.*

A train made up of many carriages, being pushed from behind by two engines, steam-driven, panting and struggling with difficulty through an ascending chain of mountains.

The white lunatics on the zoo grass; their stiffened bodies and faces. Lunacy. Paranoiacs. A kind of paralysis of the inner self. Nothing sadder than this reality. The condor will not offer to spread out his bedraggled and tawdry wings. Captivity weighs him down. Years of confinement have deadened his spirits. His eyes are filled with blood.

'*Nous fumons tous ici l'opium de la grande altitude, voix basse, petit pas, petit souffle.*' All of us smoke the opium of high altitude here, with low voices, short steps, short breaths.

And in this year alone, 1960, sixteen territories in Africa, with 85 million inhabitants, became independent.

The brunette's exercises in the nude still go on; a resplendent bare white figure exposed to the morning sun – a white goddess behind glass. Juno's love back and mesial groove.

One fine morning, looking down through the leaves and electric-blue Canterbury-bell-shaped jacaranda blossoms, from the upper deck of a number 11 bus, I recognized her below, standing in the queue, fully dressed. Very proper, wearing a belt, haughty, attractive-looking, pitch-black hair, rather stern, partly unrecognizable. Unknowable shape, living statue.

Sardines swim always towards the sun; so to catch them you must go to the east of them in the morning, and to the west of them in the afternoon.

XXXVI

A well-built young beauty in a white pleated skirt that clings to her hips and outlines her rangy thighs, a suggestion of briefs underneath, and the classic amphora-outline of the female lower torso, intimations of considerable sexual prowess, a tight fit, walking alone in Joubert Park of a summer evening.

Field research.

The handsome couple sitting on a bench under the trees in the little steeply inclined park at the top of Stuart Drive. The woman has a bouffant hairstyle, her thick black hair piled up on top of her head; she wears a dark red corded jacket and a close-fitting purple-brown tweed skirt, show-ing a lot of leg. She might be Yugoslav. The man is dressed in a dark suit with a white shirt; he might be Italian or French. They are a striking couple. A little boy of about three is with them. He stands a little way off and watches them. They are embracing. The child watches them embracing. He is told to go away and play. He goes away but soon is back again, staring at them. The woman takes him on her knees. The huddle of the three of them together. Bare trees, late evening sun, the last light dying on the mine-dumps beyond Bez Valley. Hot love 6,000 feet up. The supplicants; sure I must perish by your charms unless you take me in your arms.

Hot days; leaves falling about the Donald McKay Park, the poplars turning silver-white in the rising wind. Afternoon showers of torrential rain. Dry here all summer, now the rains come in the autumn; and every day the pictures slip a little more off square on the walls, following another fall-in down in the mines.

XXXVII   Bagley

A new man in the Scenario Department. New blood. Bagley. A small faded person in sagging trousers. He seems to be covered in a kind of grey lichen. Short strutting walk, precise manner, partly bald, with a rash of eczema on his temples, impossible to say whether his hair is his own or not; wears the one dark morning suit, bifocals, sports a goatee beard. A look of Trotsky. Very muddy complexion, and a fearful impediment in his speech. Why does Morgan hire these freaks? There are three of us in the department now, all with the same starved anxious look, and all with goatee beards. My other colleague, Egaltine, puts out occasional verse and helps to edit a magazine devoted to the arts, for the Meat Board.

55

Bagley himself deserves some space. He is an ex-journalist on the *Rand Daily Mail*. He worked for Laurence Gander. Very sanguine manner with Morgan. Exactly the wrong way to treat him. The boss, masking his venomous nature, is all politeness to him. I cannot see this state of affairs lasting. His hilarious attempts to pronounce 'Chamonix' over the telephone.

The goatee-bearded Scenario Department walking at the double after the dapper General Manager, rounding the corner of Kruis Street and disappearing into a cinema, entering a small private theatre in the bowels of the cinema, to study and comment on pre-release screenings of the department's day-to-day output. International prize-winning advertising films. I Sha-sha-sha . . . I show-show-show . . . shash-shash-shasssshsshzz . . . Chamonixer! Go to. Tongue-tied. *Tu quoque.*

Bagley's tics: one leg crossed over the other in a fussy way, agitated in the air, humming. Picking his thoughtful upper lip with a thoughtful thumb and forefinger and letting it smack back into place (signifying what?). Clicking in and out (sometimes for twenty minutes at a stretch) the retractable point of his Bic pen. Very cross-looking when contradicted – a myopic glare directed at me. Small somewhat conceited man. Omnivorous reader. A book always on his desk. *Atlas Shrugged*, by Ayn Rand.

XXXVIII   Mr Allen

An old drunken white falling off a number 11 bus at a stop in Isipingo Street. Some of the passengers reach out as if to help him. Those who are getting off have almost to jump over him. He lies there, holding his heart. Jay and a young man help him to his feet. He has hurt his head. 'Oh I have lived too long,' an old drunk of seventy-six who lies on his back on the pavement, staring up at them. 'Let me lie.'

They take him to Netherley House, a home for indigent

old men. It's some way back from the road with a forecourt of candystripe pillars, red and white, ferns, a turkey-cock scratching its wings on the cement floor, and in the background more old men hobbling about in the gloom. It's like looking into an aquarium.

Poor Bagley near tears. As suspected, tyrant Morgan has set about breaking his spirit, and with predictable results. Humiliating script conference.

Dream: the racing savage, the thick foliage, puff of gun-smoke from the tunnel in the forest. The carcass of a wild beast – boar or bear? wild hog? – being hauled out by the hind legs. Signifying what? Years' dreams return; I am another now, and yet the same.

XXXIX   A journal of the Terror

Reading a book with that title in the City Library. An account of the occurrences in the Temple during the confinement of Louis XVI, by Monsieur Cléry, the King's *valet de chambre*, together with a description of the last hours of the king by the Abbé de Firmont. Folio Society, 1955.

'We were scarcely seated when a head on the point of a pike was held to the window . . . the head was the Princess de Lamballe's, which, though bleeding, was not disfigured, and her fine light hair, still curling, waved round the pike.

The body of the Princess de Lamballe, naked and bloody as it had been dragged from the Prison de la Force to the Temple . . .

The person that carried it was mounted upon the rubbish of some houses that were ordered to be pulled down for the purpose of isolating the Tower: another stood behind, holding the heart of the unfortunate Princess, covered with blood, on the point of a sabre.'

In the massacre of September 1792, over 1,000 men and

women were done away with, some of them with great cruelty.

Bagley's departure.

XL Sharpeville

March 21st, 1960. Anti-Pass Law demonstration in Vereen-iging. The police, with Saracens in support, fired on and killed 69 African demonstrators, men and women, wounding 186.

March 24th. Smell of sickness in the deserted Sundowner Bar. Later the regulars drift in. The subdued brandy drinker orders another Commando from Richard, as he has been doing for months, years, on end. Beginning to show in his face. Immersed in his *Rand Daily Mail* as usual.

Of the 186 wounded, 38 are at Vereeniging Hospital and 148 at Baragwanath Hospital; over seventy per cent of the wounds were in the back and so terrible that it was thought dum-dum bullets were used by the police. These wounds were in fact caused by 'tumbling' bullets coming from Sten guns fired continuously without pauses between bursts.

On one of the ominous days after Sharpeville, a time of dire portents when the long-threatened seemed about to come at last, a rumour was circulating to the effect that a mob of Africans were marching from the locations on Johannesburg. The old woman, Anna, our washerwoman from Orlando, I knew was in the flat with Jay; I decided not to phone, and went back to work.

Morgan, who prided himself on his fair treatment of his own African servants, had an automatic pistol out on his desk and some rounds of ammunition. 'If I have to go,' he said, mock-histrionic, 'I'll take some of them with me.' His secretary scuttled from the room. 'Oh, Mr Mor-GAN!'

The rest of that peculiar day. The feeling that we were on the edge of civil war, that one might perhaps not live beyond tomorrow, that Jay and the child would die, was like a hand of ice.

After work the city cleared fast, a rapid exodus to the suburbs, leaving the centre of the city deserted. African newspaper boys were flying through the streets on their bicycles and flinging down the late editions at the feet of the remaining white bus queues, like insolent pages come from the enemy lines with bold ultimatums.

But the *Star* reported nothing of an undisciplined horde marching on Johannesburg, no picture of the bloodied head of the Princess de Lamballe on the end of a pike; it reported only common everyday occurrences. The beautiful Miss Antoinette Botha photographed at the pottery exhibition of Henk Jacobs and Harry Duys.

On the way home, the bored tennis coach, still in flannels and peaked cap, still lobbing brown tennis balls over a net at the municipal hard courts to a very unaccomplished male novice at the game.

XLI Glissade

April 21st. A month after Sharpeville, and the blood-stains still on the road. I ask Lewis Nkose, 'What kind of man is Colonel Spengler?' 'Spengler?' he says. 'He is a butcher. He has the face of a butcher.'

He speaks of the sweetish smell of blood that you could smell, after the shooting. He was there.

The air is full of flying mine-dust. I have an inflamed throat and retire to bed at about nine, feeling wretched. Mourning air of forgotten childhood mingled with premonitions of one's last end. Evening Benediction begins; night falls, out of the craters rise the mists. Knowing nothing, believing nothing; live a little longer, if you can. I have this disturbing dream: I am flying in the Alps with six others. We are dressed as for skiing. Our arms extended, like gliders we fly about in the thin rarefied air, our shadows following us below on the virgin snow. It's high up in the Alps. I am there, drifting about. Someone calls, 'Feel the snow! It's like fire.' I sail down and kick up some with my bare feet. Yes, like fire.

There is a high escarpment that no one can clear. I attempt it, but it's impossible, the face is too steep.

In the Alpine hut one of the party has cut himself by accident. There's not much blood, but nevertheless he says he must return to the base. He leaves immediately. A pair of scissors lies on the table. I take them up and cut myself deeply on both wrists. Great clots of blood stain the walls and the snow near the door. I've severed an artery; the blood goes on pumping out. I am weakening; it's I who have done this, yet I seem to be standing outside myself. I watched 'myself' do it: 'him' I take for myself.

A Johannesburg *Star* photograph of the 'weapons' used by the African insurgents at Sharpeville. In 40–45 seconds of firing, so many killed, so many wounded, so much blood. A pile of knobkerries, sticks, stones. Like what?

Windfalls in a winter wood.

PART THREE

The Islands

July 21st, 1960. Last day in Johannesburg. Main railway terminal. Train for Blaney and East London. We sail from there on the 28th. I read of ten Africans killed and four injured, three seriously, in a faction fight between Mbonos and Ngulubenis at Maritzburg.

The taciturn soldier. Kliptown, Midway, Lenz, the locations out of Johannesburg. A week's holiday in King William's Town ahead. Jay has gone ahead there to her parents three weeks previously.

Kidd's Beach, Eastern Province. We rent a house near the beach. The breathing of the cattle at night. Generally deserted beaches. The coloured youths dancing like dervishes naked on the dunes; their swaying stallions' erections. The two African girls coming in their city finery. They all go swimming together. Scrummages in the surf. Their cries.

The lagoon. Deep coughing of the baboons among the laurels. Days alone there. The dog swimming in the estuary early in the morning. The Bantu girls coming with their fancy-men. Putty-coloured skin of the Cape Malays, with deformed features, like lepers. In the evening we buy brandy, for 15s. a bottle.

Jay's dream: 'It's a big hotel next to the railway lines. My mother and I have a big room on the second floor. I'm trying to pack but she keeps on emptying the suitcase. She is discontented and moves from room to room spreading the clothes about.

'On our side of the building and directly in front of the

63

hotel four oil tanks stand, delicate quadrupeds with their four big balls on the top standing about a hundred feet off the ground.

'There's a revolution in the city. The first oil tank is set on fire above our heads. It explodes in flames. There is a terrific outcry in the hotel, with guests screaming out of windows and running through the rooms. I run to my mother, but she is so petulant she doesn't care. I look everywhere for the suitcase. She's hidden it. I ask her where it is; she says she doesn't know. I hear people running past the hotel and shouts outside. Then I find the suitcase. I begin to pack in a hurry. My mother keeps taking the clothes out and throwing them on the bed.

'The second oil tank is now on fire. I hear the roaring of the flames and black particles of steel and ash are falling past the windows. Try as I can, the suitcase always remains empty. Outside, we see the flames going straight up. There was a man there. I knew he was there. I shout to a friend to go and help him. There are two of them after him, and I can see him clearly lying on his stomach under the third oil tank, which he is about to set on fire.

'As he reaches up he is shot from behind through the back of the head. Dying, he goes on making the gesture of pulling a lever, unmindful that it's someone else who moves his hand.'

July 28th, 1960, East London docks. The *Warwick Castle* berthed. An easy customs check, and we go to a small cabin, uncomfortably so with a collapsible cot installed. Some telegrams from Johannesburg are waiting for us. We will be cooped up here for the next eighteen days, with smells of decaying fruit and damp ammonia-smelling diapers. Sailing via St Helena and Ascension Island to Tilbury, England.

Port Elizabeth. A liner, pearly-grey hull, entering a harbour early in the morning. A seaweed-covered breakwater, a sludge of fog, a ship sounding its horn, and in the dampness on the mole fifty Moslems in red fezzes standing waiting, hardly human, like diver-birds grouped on a rock. Suddenly handkerchiefs appear in their hands and are limply waved about their heads in silence, still not very enthusiastic.

The silence and vastness of the liner making its way slowly into the harbour. Its tiers of deserted decks; chill of the hour, just before daybreak.

Capetown. The Moslems in full regalia posing, very patient, for amateur photographers on D Deck in a thin drizzle of rain. The ship's nurse orders them about. They are Cape coloureds, Moslems returning to Capetown after a nine-month trip to Mecca.

Low cloud over the city, Table Mountain invisible; smoke rising from the business quarters, joined up to low-hanging discoloured clouds – like a city after a bombardment. The persistent thin rain. Two tugs pulling the *Warwick Castle* off its berth. The harbour turns round. The tugs cast off. Music over the ship's loudspeakers; the wake stretches out behind. Now we leave this continent; now the ship sails. Feeling of elation.

. . . A day out and the Cape rollers begin. Vomit on the companionway mats, the dining-room half empty, and the Belgian Congolese children yelling: *'Malade! Malade!'*

Two days out and already bored with shipboard life. St Helena in the morning. I wrote to Mr Solomen (or Solomens) there; his grandfather sold macaroni to Napoleon.

St Helena. Discoloured volcanic cliffs, then the valley, and Jamestown, with boats coming out. We are to stay here until evening. I see a high waterfall coming down, white water, and more boats putting out from the island. Festive appearance. The islanders come on board to sell trinkets. I talk to one of the young men. He herds sheep; he brought some from the back of the island at five this morning. His sing-song voice. Biblical scene.

The young men are leaving the island, he tells me, to work on the American air-bases on Ascension. They made an air-strip along the ridge of a volcanic mountain. They can double their wages there, working in radio. The jute factories pay little. Those who stay are attempting to start a trade-union movement – the first in the island's history. They load jute into the hold. It has a bad smell. Some of the older islanders are going into domestic service in Scotland. A butler and housekeeper. He is small, scorched black by the sun, his sing-song English difficult to follow.

I go ashore with another passenger – a white-haired, stout, elderly Chinaman, very polite and formal. Mr Johns. Very courteous, neatly dressed in a blue suit with a white shirt and dark tie, a raincoat over one arm, a rolled umbrella in his hand (what Chinaman would go without an umbrella?). He carries an expensive attaché case, as an emblem of caste? We introduce ourselves. He tells me he was born on St Helena but left it as a young man to seek his fortune in the USA. He worked for fifty years as a traveller in the Bible trade, married an American lady from Boston, Mass., and is now retired. He is through with the Bible business. He had hoped to spend his last years on the island, but his wife does not care for it – not enough social contact, too many white ants, insufficient refrigeration. They had originally planned to live on the island for three years, in a sort of trial retirement, but no, his wife couldn't stand it; they are leaving again in the spring. He himself would have liked to have stayed, but he would do what his wife wanted; she would never be happy there. They plan to return to Boston.

He introduces me to Pastor Phillips, from Orlando location, Johannesburg, on the steps of Jamestown PO. I too am from Jo'burg. Orlando!

I make an arrangement to meet Mr Johns later with Jay (who has stayed on board with the child); we are to take a taxi and visit Longwood House. I take leave of him on a small humpback Chinese bridge, surrounded by white

66

blossoms, with the sound of water trickling in the irrigation streams, no sound of human voices in this quiet backward island retreat a thousand miles from anywhere, and take a walk up the valley – glad to be off the ship.

The *Warwick Castle*, much diminished, lying offshore about three-quarters of a mile out, seen between two converging cliffs.

Terraces sown with peas and beans, warm dry air, hot sunshine, peace. An outdated greeting to Princess Elizabeth and Prince Philip painted on a hillside. A rustic England of the early nineteenth century perpetuated here. With an annual rainfall of thirty-six inches, a very temperate climate; one could live 1,700 feet above sea level in a temperature of seventy degrees all the year round.

Longwood House in the afternoon. Napoleon's last resting-place, a long way from the frozen rivers and corpse-strewn plains of the lost Russian campaign. The cold names of the rivers that flow into the Baltic – Vistula, Niemen. Niemen-on-the-ice. Bonaparte getting into a closed carriage with his mameluke at Smorgony, defeated and on his way back to Paris. 'Halted at Jaffa at the western entrance to Asia, and halted at Moscow at the northern gateway to the same continent, he was to go and die among the seas bordering that part of the world where mankind and the sun were born.'

In the billiard-room the pockets are rotting from the table, the green baize turning white with age; the billiard balls in their wooden frames rest behind glass in the hall. Chipped antique objects – the emperor's cannons.

The smallness of his bed; its green canopy – a child's bed. His death-mask cast in bronze stands on a pedestal. Effigies of him in every room and in the hall. Vain as Voltaire.

St Helena lies between the two poles. 'At the extremity of our hemisphere,' says Tacitus, 'one can hear the sound made by the sun sinking in the sea: *sonum insuper immergentis audiri.*' When Napoleon went out, his spirits low, he passed along stony paths lined with aloes and scented broom.

In the narrow valley known then as Slane or Geranium Valley, and now as Tomb Valley, there is a spring at which Napoleon's Chinese servants, as faithful as Camões's Javanese, used to fill their pitchers; weeping willows hang over their spring; green grass, studded with champacs, grows all around. ('The champac,' says the Sanskrit poems, 'for all its colour and perfume, is not a sought after flower, because it grows on graves.')

Napoleon liked the willows by the spring, but everything saddened him under a sky beneath which life seemed shorter, the sun remaining three days less in that hemisphere than in ours. Towards the end of February 1821, in his sixth year of exile on the rock, he was obliged to take to his bed ('How low I have fallen! . . . I have stirred up the whole world, and I cannot lift my eyelids!'), and he did not get up again. He died in Longwood on May 5th, 1821. 'He sleeps like a hermit or a pariah in a valley, at the end of a deserted pathway,' wrote Chateaubriand.

In 1840 the remains were brought home to France – he had come home to be buried in the grime of Paris. Bonaparte passed through the tomb, as he passed through everything, without stopping.

Vague feeling that he did live there once; pined away and died there; written of by de Seguar, Chateaubriand, latterly Kafka, fascinated by the horrors of the Russian campaign. Suffered from migraine, dysuresis (retention of the urine). Murat, Ney; carnage at Borodino, blood-soaked fields. He had drilled peepholes in the window shutters to spy on the English soldiers going on and off duty. At daybreak here, forgotten. Never forgotten.

The lazy Azores; three miles of sea below us. The English clergyman's anaemic full-grown son in the dining-room. 'Oh of course they're not trustworthy as pets.' Finicky English voice – that strange, slight talk which governed the British Empire. 'I never take liberties with an Alsatian.' The English ladies opposite us; their movements, talk, complacency – their security. Lily Briscoe. Walking on the upper deck. Beginning of an overcast day. The jet fighter from Ascension, island of ashes, a pinpoint, then directly over the mast, then four miles out to sea.

The Canary Islands; Las Palmas. One can smell it approaching; the stench of colonial Spain.

Generalissimo Franco causeway. The taxi ride. In the cathedral the old waxen-faced priest high up in an alcove reading his office – an image from Goya. The confessional stained black about the grille: sins (bad breath?) of generations of humble penitents. An island of bad teeth and halitosis. Smells of cheap Cognac and wine gone sour in the bars. A vegetable market, white colonnades and green trellis, all the charm of Spain.

Fish-tinning factories; the Coca-Cola factory under construction on the hill. An island inundated with Japanese-made merchandise with falsified US trade-marks. Populated caves in the dirty hills above the town. The well-dressed tout offering us a Parker pen made in Osaka; another in the cathedral, shows us the manuscript Vulgate of 1614.

Hot idle days. The tourist-class swimming pool with two feet of water, Belgian Congolese children splashing in it, screaming snipe. Shrouded cars on the fore-deck with Belgian Congo registration plates. Exodus from the troubled Congo.

Circular intimations of calamity. 'The contemporary of Napoleon conceived his completion of European philosophy as the fulfilment of a primary undeveloped origin. The contemporary of Adolf Hitler conceives the identical history of the European spirit as the gradual epiphany of Nihilism.'* So what of Father Adam and his teeming billions of posterity.

The weather turns foul; heavy seas, troughs of grey waves. A porthole, a stretch of harbour, docks of Las

* Hans Magnus Enzensberger

Palmas, a boat loading up alongside the *Warwick Castle*, a view of burnt hills, already only a memory.

Two portholes; slothful slop and wallow of the waves striking the side of the ship; grey-green sea agitated all the way to the horizon. Staring before her with empty eyes.

The tarpaulin-shrouded cars on deck. Hardly any place to exercise now. We left Europe four years ago with frightened Germans leaving after the Hungarian Uprising; we are going back to Europe with Belgians running from the Belgian Congo.

A dance on the upper deck at night. The engine-driver from Rhodesia, bluff bonhomie. Thrust of the prow. The captain's warm handclasp. Cole Porter's 'Night and Day'.

The English Channel.

We reach the mouth of the Thames in the late afternoon, but can't get into Tilbury. There's a dock strike on (also a printing strike).

When we wake up next morning we're in. Through the portholes we see English bobbies standing about with their hands behind their backs on the wet dockside. It's raining in grey Tilbury.

Berlin Days and Nights
LETTERS FROM LINDERMANN

1969–70

If things seem not to be as once they were
Perhaps they are as once they seemed to be.

C. H. Sisson

Aberam Abend

Evenings in Nullgrab – the empty grave of West Berlin –
are long; Chateaubriand remarked upon it. Shop signs are
distinctive, don't ask me why; you know you are in
Germany. Is it the neon blue of Schultheiss beer, or the
strong evidence of old *Sütterlin*? Change your script, change
the *Gestalt*; still hoping for a change of heart.

The symbols for cities vary. For Nullgrab, a bear. Dr
Franz Kafka began his death here, hard by the Botanic
Gardens. The loves of his life were Felice Bauer, Milena
Jesenská, Dora Dymant of this city.

Situated between the rivers Elbe and Oder, the former
capital fell to the Red Armies of the USSR on May 2nd,
1945, just over three centuries after the Thirty Years War;
almost a century and a half after the Seven Years War.

The Russians removed the Pergamon Gate, the Istar Gate
of Babylon, took in its entirety Hoppenhaupt's Silver Room
from its Potsdam Neues Palais; left the *Siegessäule*, Müggel-
turm, volle Pulle, kept Köpenick.

Evenings in Nullgrab are endless.

As an eight-year-old schoolboy, Vladimir Nabokov had
braces put in his teeth here, wrote later: 'There are little
cul-de-sacs where at dusk the soul seems to dissolve.' He
went skating here, through the blue-grey dissolving Berlin
dusk, as did Jules Laforgue half a century before. Arnold
Schoenberg was born here.

A hawk flies down Schlüterstrasse in the rain, by the
Hotel Bogotá, a blackbird sings in Fasanenstrasse.

Der Lump (*der Grofaz*)

No longer will he (the Devastator: *der Verwüstende*) send out those iron-fisted *Diktat*s phrased with such elegance. Over the ruins of Nullgrab, for requiem, came Bruckner's Ninth, something by Wagner. As for the same Bruckner, who had been regarded by his own contemporaries as a total fool, few composers have been so unpretentious about their work. He dedicated his Ninth to '*dem lieben Gott*'; never finished it. The Viennese fool steered clear of court jesters, was absurdly devoted to the lesser Wagner. A rural type, universities despised him, the critics too – 'Bruckner composes like a drunkard.'

He was given to extensive eating and beer-swilling, after the manner of Zille the great cartoonist. Garlic and dirty clothes, slowly getting old, that was Bruckner. Aristocratic ladies avoided him.

Dr Zondyke

Dr Zondyke is almost two metres tall and makes a lot of noise. His family was liquidated by the Nazis. He likes to tell the story of their fate (he himself the only survivor) for the thousandth time, while engaged in medical research and sending off articles that nobody wants to read.

Academic diseases (Professor Hartnung)

Affable Professor Hartnung is strange and growing obsessive, engaged in '*Aktensammeln*', total foolishness, and what amounts to double-dealing, hidden vanity disguised (thinly) as humility, always at the back doors of whatever kind of folly one finds in literature and its surroundings, among practitioners, critics, spoilers of any kind of common sense, humour, fun; the pseudos skilfully spreading their germs, the Almighties with their false aims, false ways of thinking and talking, disturbing peoples' minds with their unsound ways of chopping logic – 'Psychotropic Lit.'.

Stout Hugo

Stout Hugo is American, a painter who also dubs German porn movies into basic English: *The Secret Sex Life of the Three Musketeers*. That hog is eating his greasy way around the town. Wherever you go, there will he be over a dish of some exotic food, in the company of 'important' beings, introducing them with his full, rich, sonorous voice. Little brains, hoggish heart. Paints military subjects in veal colours.

Kurzgarten, Fischerhüttenstrasse

Many old people are found in the Kurzgarten now, down the way from Krumme Lanke. They order *Kaffee und Kuchen*. They are addicted to this.

It is somehow fashionable to laugh at them, all the old ladies who have seen so many things. I wish that they will not be run over.

Am writing this in the Kurzgarten on a warm day in Nullgrab, since so long ago, sitting at the window, watching the exotic tree with the bean-like flowers, and drinking chilled Mosel as we have tasted it here before. You are sitting opposite me, smoking a Daneman cigar and scratching your beard. Down the way, as you know, the lakes begin, tributaries of the old Quellfluss.

The ever-perambulating opera-singer still sings wordless mezzo-soprano arias in the Grunewald. French divers still search for parts of the Lancaster bomber in the brown deeps of Krumme Lanke.

The Forbidden Ground

Marxist Professors on GDR channels discuss us like doctors, stating the disease, Capitalist Cancer, with sparkling eyes. No anarchist station, no contrast to that dull programme, no Cioran, Stirner – banished to the universities and the recital halls.

AFN is surreal. That remorselessly fidgety American (commercial) way of chopping up time, commercial 'slots' on the airwaves from the far-off Land of the Fast Buck. The rape victim's plea sounds like another plug. Brashness here, high hopes, syncopated 'optimism'.

Vague humanism from the Marxists. Utopianism. Very cold and very good in old Nullgrab. Lightning, by a secret arrangement, always passes our borders, never comes in.

Volksfest

We move slow and are still waiting for you. But now we often go for a drink to the big *Volksfest*, where we sit in a saloon drinking Pabst Blue Ribbon beer, very cold and very good.

Sometimes I am awfully bored with all these poor substitutes for nature here, the parks and small grey lakes. It is a dull day, and I have nothing of any importance to tell you.

Herr Kunoth

Herr Kunoth the *Hausmeister* is clipping the bushes behind the blocks of flats in Prinzregentenstrasse where we used to drink Kalte Ente with Anneliese in the old days. Everything ready for spring, except Lindermann.

Gedächtniskirche

Gedächtniskirche is a smelly place. There was a pool of piss in front of the plaque, hippies and bums having a good exhibition time on the steps during the warm months, one pissing merrily away in the ruins next to embarrassed camera-laden tourists. I saw no bride in white leaving in a white carriage drawn by white horses.

Berlin Days and Nights

Irmgard Hecht

Our landlady Irmgard Hecht, back from China, gives monster lantern-slide lectures arranged after her last voyage. She knows the world, goes with the Red Cross Board to faraway places. This time it was Red China.

There was a photo of today's Shanghai, a narrow street crowded with people performing gynastic exercises. Fräulein Hecht was very impressed. The order of the streets, the health of the masses, the 'almost Prussian' way of handling things.

Old pattern, I am sorry to say; it dies hard. She used to be a *glühende* Nazi, now calls Willy Brandt a gangster. All kinds of lunatics currently inhabit Haus Hecht. The old widow in black who is in mourning for thirty years now for her daughter, Rotraut Richter, star of *Veilchen vom Potsdamer Platz*, a famous old weepy movie of those times.

The blonde radio-announcer falls downstairs almost nightly. A French couple in the basement, cuisine with much garlic. Felix (my cat) sometimes smelling of garlic when he comes in at night; suppose they leave their window open.

'Hallo, Herbst, du wirst chic!'

Autumn, and a very 'classic' one here in Nullgrab, is a strict time for me. Turning away from the worthless life that brought me not what I had expected of it, the pictures that interest me, the world of fantasy like the mad boy's in *Le Sud* (you preferred the sister, if I remember well); throwing away reality, finding a new one. I cannot express it well enough.

I have been in Italy, and since returning have spread cholera all over Nullgrab. I had a rather restricted holiday, three weeks during which I had intended to move around a bit, but *basta finito* because of that ancient disease (you die saltless, they say, covered with vomit and shit) that kept creeping up north, so I did not take any chances and stayed around Venice most of the time.

What can you do there but swim and play ping-pong? Crowds of Germans playing skat and drinking beer into the early morning. Frankfurters and natives of Stuttgart employ the oddest diminutives: '*Grüss Gott, Gottle, Gut's Nächtle!*'

Fellow from Manchester – worst accent I ever heard. A young Jew from Poland thrown out by Gomułka, with relatives scattered all over the world, supplying him money which he used to buy himself company, telling the most interesting lies all day long.

Met many swindlers of all calibres, parking their futuristic cars (hired?) in front of the old Adriatic Grand Hotels, all carrying small handbags like ninnies. Italian girls, however, are not very easy to impress; proud and sportive, with short-cut curly black hair, speeding away on small motorbikes.

I had a slow-motion holiday all the way. Finally got rid of some strange headaches I had for quite a time, shadows of my (dirty) last year.

Waidmann

Walter Waidmann resides in Steglitz, former 'brown district' with still many of the grim Nazi villas standing behind high walls. Didn't Wordsworth have a theory that houses should be the same colour as the land they stand on? In some primitive cultures human dwellings are glued together with excrement.

Nuremburg

There is a drill ground in Nuremburg extensive enough to accommodate two million men. The concrete approach is in three sixteen-inch steps, one above the other, stretching for a mile or so. The entire field is enclosed with high embankments and towers. *He* addressed them there. How beautiful you are, *meine Germanen*, he told them. *Ach*, the dark varnish of public moralizing! Numbers went to his head, crowds stimulated him, rage seemed to suit him: he chewed rugs, threw fits, danced when Paris fell.

In the *Bunker*, at the end, he told his English secretary that the world was not yet ready for National Socialism; it would have to wait another 2,000 years. He liked to think globally, and in millennia.

Of ruined, bombed Nuremburg, Rebecca West wrote during the trial: 'It was typically apocalyptic. There was something like a regiment buried under the ruins of the old town, and when the wind stirred it brought you an extraordinary stench of decaying regiment and disinfectant. There was acre after acre of ruined Nuremburg and you would suddenly be faced – without any explanation – with a vast head of God, cut off at the neck and left lying on the pavement: they had no time to tidy it up. It was the most terrible Last Day Michaelangelesque scene of desolation. The trial was quite fantastic in many ways and it was so strange to find it was overwhelmingly American.'

Not any more.

The grid patterning of big modern cities is modelled upon nineteenth-century American, except that the grid unit has sides 2,000 yards long. Into each square could be fitted any of the great cities of the past. Florence for instance.

Karin

Karin the gangster's young moll was thrown out of maternity home for disobeying orders and chain-smoking, baby and all. The putative father has been released from jail but still faces a trial for robbery in Frankfurt. He is earning his money by cheating at card games and, very likely, as a pimp. Huge grey guy, very brutal; with him, one should drink only Coca-Cola. He worries much about Karin's past, phoned one of her former boyfriends late one night, promising to cut off his penis.

Institutional misery

The *Klinikum* (or does one say *Krankenhaus*) that stands back in its own grounds on Fisherhüttenstrasse near Krumme Lanke *U-Bahn*, being the end of the line, has garden and evergreen glades lending an elegiac cemetery mood to the surroundings, enhanced by the pale faces of incurable convalescents peering from upper windows, or sitting in dressing-gowns on garden seats, or moving slowly about, lethargic as flies in winter, all hope and most life drained out of them. Live for the hour.

Wannseebad

The sand of this man-made beach is fine as salt, shifted from Nordsee shores. Let the time be 6.15 p.m. on a calm blue early July evening in 1970 (how time flies back!). Water temperature 20; air 15. Two fellows wading, one he-man, one bald. A rubbery lady breast-stroking for distant Kladow. Scum of bread along the shore. Swans. Their ill-tempered hissing, sigh of the waves, mostly wake of *Motorschiff Vaterland* bound for Spandau, or *Dampfer Siegfried* pushing towards the Wannsee landing-stage. All in good order.

Back off the beach, in the sandy playground, two teenage girls on the swings, calling, throwing their legs up, laughing. Their cries. Joy.

An incoming jet laying a vapour trail towards Tempelhof. Movements of air, water, clouds, girlish limbs, brown. Life.

All converge, all disperse; reassemble only to disperse again. Figure me there.

Fontane

Aiming at precision of dialect, just to get the gist of it, what for example do you make of Fontane's *Der Stechlin*, if anything?

Do you understand the servant Joseph's Yorkshire dialect in *Wuthering Heights*? Can you whistle me a few bars of Mozart's *King Thamos*? Precisely. And what do you think of the Cioran *mot*, 'Why read Plato, if a saxophone can give you an idea of another world?'

Music: a system of farewells. And the Germans are most addicted to it.

Lichtenrade light

A hawk passes a bedroom window of the Hotel Bogotá in Schlüterstrasse. Outside, a blue evening has fallen. The early prostitutes have begun parading on the Ku'damm. Traffic rages up and down. Images of security elsewhere, well-to-do urban life: summer light in Lichtenrade, Zehlendorf evenings, open space in Marienfelde, wheat around the village of Lübars.

Evening falls. Nullgrab does not exist. City of Max Klante, the Skylanke brothers, Bernotat the bibliomaniac, the notorious Sass brothers. Snowbound city of Zille. Now, today, this evening, the ever-jovial drinker of Doornkat raises his glass and invites you to imbibe. Nullgrab only half exists.

Herr Carsten of Lichterfelde lies buried in a small district cemetery, having expired in a state of insanity in woody Schöneberg's Maison de Santé – Schöneberg being the district he despised most, now better known for its rash of stinking pizzerias.

In Zehlendorf's peaceful Waldfriedhof, Erich Hinüber (Erich all-over) sleeps his last sleep, with Rille and Nille, Dattel and Ding, Mose and Orgel. With Kitzler and Klemme, who were whelped there, also Zitternadel and Schwanzklammer, not to mention Saftpresser and Zwicke.

Brief I

Belated congratulations on your birthday and many thanks for your letter. Have been walking all day in bright sunshine, seventeen degrees centigrade and the air has an earthy smell in Lichtenrade, where I would like to live some day without a telephone and travel downtown whenever I feel like it. I drink to your health.

The wine reminds me of the best name of all those names Thomas Mann invented: Müller-Rose, the second-rate actor in *Felix Krull*. Walking here and there, misguidedly, as if inspired by the *genius loci* of the place. A city difficult to imagine but, once seen, never forgotten. Blind Borges called it the ugliest city on earth. But it's only half a city, at the best. It is our modern world.

Gottfried Benn

Gottfried Benn estimated towards the end of his life that he had earned from writing poetry some 400DM, or scarcely enough to keep a keen cigar-smoker in cigars for a year. (I am thinking now of your favourite *bête noire*, Professor Bernie Knell.)

His (Benn's) real trade was venereal diseases. He had a practice in Bozenerstrasse, in lovely Schöneberg.

An elderly couple called the Schroders have already chosen a grave-plot next to that of Benn in Zehlendorf; no finer example of German (Prussian?) snobbery extending into or beyond *das Grab* could be found. It was Benn who wrote to a friend: 'Sometimes for an hour you *are*, the rest is history; sometimes the two floods culminate in a dream.' What did he mean? The Germans are a people apt to believe in their own destiny; *Schicksal* soon becoming *Schnicksal*.

Schwäbisch

Schwäbisch is a Low German dialect, prone to diminutives, peculiar to Stuttgart, Tübingen, Baden-Württemberg and the Black Forest.

Nullgrabers young and old are notorious for inventing

names of derision; they are most prolific at this, having made an art of it.

Nullgrab *Steppke* (Zille's offspring).

Reading Ned Ward's *London Spy*. Danced at *Fasching* party with girl disguised as a polar bear.

Jagdschloss, Grunewald

There be many a spooky spot in the Grunewald, but the spookiest of all is the old Jagdschloss itself. Joachim II's bewitching servant-maid *die schöne Giesserin*, loved and lost, was probably immured alive in the cellar. Her civil name was Anna Sydow.

At dead of stormy nights she puts on all the lights in the Hunting Lodge and dances alone to unearthly music, mindful of the old days, favours conferred, the love of Joachim.

All at once the doors and windows swing open by themselves. In the kitchen the grills start revolving as if moved by *Geist*s. Candlelight throws the shadows of hunters over walls and ceiling and long-dead horses are heard neighing in the empty stables. Sometimes the old master of the wine-cellar – depicted in stone, as you would recall, by the entrance door – carrying an enormous bunch of keys, joins Anna Sydow. And if the night is an extremely stormy one, old Kunz *Buntschuh*, the insane court jester, joins them, laughing dementedly.

Legends of the Grunewald

Albrecht der Bär is chasing Jaczo, the Wendish Prince, whose Gods have forsaken him.

Jaczo arrives at the Havel. He prays to the Christian God for the first time, begging for help. Already he hears the shouts of his pursuers. Closing on him they call out: '*Jetzt haben wir ihn im Sack!*'

Now his horse, hearing 'Now we have him in the sack',

whinnies and jumps into the Havel, then considered a most dangerous stretch of water. The horse drowns from exhaustion but Jaczo is safe. He puts his horn and his shield down and falls on his knees to pray.

The spot where his horse jumped is still called Sack; the place where Jaczo put down his horn and shield still called Schildhorn. For a long time a pillar stood there with the Wendish shield; it was formed like a tree trunk with a cross on top.

The drowned church

A fisherman once drew up his net from the bottom of Grunewaldsee. It snagged; he heard underwater church bells. The sun burst through the clouds, revealing to him a church sunken in the lake. He jumped overboard with a wild shout and was seen no more.

At times thereafter a lonely fisherman is greatly alarmed to see a church steeple rising from the waves with a fishing-net entangled on the spire.

Brief II

Spent New Year's Eve at home listening to heavy rainfall and sounds of misfired fireworks. Natives bought vast supply and suffered many casualties.

Sometimes we meet in your old Alma Mater, the dark Annapam Bar near Arnimallee. We talk of you.

Felix the cat caught mice twice and finished them off under the bath as usual. (Recommended reading: Poe's 'Veil of the Soul'.) Here in Nullgrab we have had spring weather for two months now. Willows budding, primroses in full blossom, Herr Kunoth dead of a heart-attack. *Blatt* headliner: 'WITH LILACS, DAISIES INTO THE NEW YEAR!' The Atika couple in a renewed frenzy of buying. Hedgehogs in a daze move slowly about the gardens, finding no sleep. Early infants and fat worms, bird fanfares in the city of Döblin and Grosz, today.

Möhring *und Krume*

At Potsdam by the Havel, *Grossmutti* waits for ever, the coffee for her skating grandchildren undrinkable in the cup, the *Brötchen* long eaten by the crows, her outstretched arms become branches. Potsdam lies within the Forbidden Ground. *Verboten* to skate there today on the frozen Havel. The grandchildren grown up, moved elsewhere.

Herr Hund

Genial host Baldur Braun throws a beer party for the unspeakable Horst Udet, windy Sartoris, beery and hairy Herr Hund the deer-slayer. This motley and verbose company assembles at Braun's place. Host and Udet put out a local news-sheet, Marxist in tone (what Grass calls 'weekend insurrectionism'), perhaps to atone for the past, when both were SS men in the death-camps. Rumpelstilzchen dancing around the secret fire?

Kneipen

Himmelfahrt, May 8th, twenty-fifth anniversary of capitulation of German armed forces. Month of Buddha's birthday.

Many drunken *Herren* staggering in Grunewald when I went there this morning. Even drunker *Herren* returning on *Kremsers* (horse-wagons?) when yours truly walked soberly home at dusk through a copse of silver beech, spongy underfoot, hearing them singing, hoarsely and most unmelodiously, on Königin-Luise-Strasse; and do not remember VE day of twenty-five years ago, day of speeches and political promises, on Germany's desecrated soil. *More* dark varnish.

Speaking of desecration – when the Youth Leader's first son was born unto Frau Baldur von Schirach, to the strains of Caruso's '*La donna è mobile*', it was ordained that a full shovelful of good German soil be sent from each province, to spread it under the babe's cradle and pay homage to the august name of von Schirach.

Reichsminister Dr Goebbels (The Gnome), *Gauleiter* of Nullgrab, being a poetic type, sent a paving-stone.

This city exists for me. The Russians annexed the eastern (Prussian) regions, Brandenburg included; the core states are now absorbed into the Forbidden Ground. Nullgrab itself is a land island of 341 square miles, a hundred miles inside the GDR.

Inflation between the wars produced gangsters of the snatcher (*Raffke*) type, the Sass brothers being the most successful bank-robbers.

Meanwhile Hugo the stout Texan is systematically eating his way around town.

Nullgrab parties

Nullgrab parties are crowded with multicoloured monsters and strangely feathered birds, including Indians and the inevitable Wild Irishman who sits broodingly in a corner, casting wild glances about as he is expected to; that green bog of obelisks and follies still being very much *à la mode*, many young people going there to discover another of their 'great things'. The Dubliners roar out 'Yur dhrunnk! Yurrdhhrunnkkk!!' most poshlustily.

Natürlich!

On Krumme Lanke a naturist female no longer young, with the browned-off lethargic appearance peculiar to nudists, is removing her small bikini, scrubbing her sagging udders, smiling winsomely at me.

The *Bullenwinkel* is elsewhere, by the Hunting Lodge and

the *Hund*-Bathing-Place. I spy it from the opposite shore: the look of a military encampment with a cutting-back of trees, an opening-out of glades. No breeze stirs the cropped pines. An elderly male nudist attired in black socks is sunning his back and withered shanks. The young male nudists are an unhappy cross between Crusoe and Stone Age Man, with something of Charles Manson. Cries carry over the lake. *Ferdi! Anna! Mutti! Horst!*

Heavy bouncing dogs, lightly bouncing *Knaben*. Blue plastic refuse-containers on the slopes produce a regulated look; *Ordnung* reinforced by the slow approach of a small blue-black police-car now crawling like a bug over the hill. Same revolver-blue as the beetles devoured by the ravenous red ants teeming on paths of the Grunewald.

Now an obese naturist mother is bending to bathe a nudist child, watched by seven Mansons with crazy fixed stares. The lunatic solemnity of the bathing, the ministering hands; the monstrous behind spreading, far from Mother Nature's open glades. As though trapped (inert, dead) in a photo; Nature in full retreat.

A breeze blowing from the right hand stirs the stripped pines. The police-bug crawls out of sight over the hill.

Ferdi!!

Difficult to *like* the Germans, sometimes. Hard to classify nice people. German rudeness is peculiar to itself, as is French rudeness, or English rudeness for that matter (the cut, oblique and direct). After all – though this is hardly the critical point – Germans are probably no worse than other tribes. I am trying to remember what Wittgenstein said about national character; have a vague idea that it was very accurate but have forgotten and am too lazy to look it up now; I think he assumed it doesn't exist at all.

Fidelity, Heine observed, fidelity – you would think they had invented it, and the Prussians the truest of all, on Bleibtreustrasse. Loyalty, a tag to cover up the moral nakedness; or the last firm ground to which self-respect could retreat? So Albert Speer, the only regretting Nazi, noted in his secret Spandau diary.

The Nameless One

No matter what time of day I venture out, to run into him
I am sure to, this nameless one, *Der Namenlose*, foreigner
(Serb or Croat) looking as if just out of bed (in the late
afternoon?), not exactly fresh, quite the contrary, tousled
and stale, with scum on his lips, gummy-eyed. His hind-
quarters positively slink along like a hyena's. *Der Namenlose*
is now about to descend an endless flight of steps leading
nowhere.

Where he goes nobody knows. Brother! *Nichts für ungut*.
The calm evening light casts the reflections of trees down
into Schlachtensee (Gunge Pond) and onto its sister lake
Krumme Lanke, in the profoundly dark depths of which a
French diver is groping in the mud for parts of a Lancaster
bomber, the bones of the RAF crew gone down all those
years ago.

We pass without formal salutation. What could we say?
Silent as the grave he passes. Yesterday I passed him on the
Rehwiese, the sunken meadows. The day before that
outside Nikolassee *S-Bahn*. Tomorrow, as like as not, on
Schopenhauerstrasse or Im Dol, or Podbielski-Allee. He is
everywhere. *L'Ignoto*, Herr Aporia, The Unknown One.

Fiend

The keep-fit fiends run around the two lakes in singlets
and tennis shoes, trailing behind them an acrid stench of
exertful German sweat. A red-headed fellow on a bicycle
blows a bugle. I walk there as if new-risen in a dream.

When I walk by the lakes, these two little lakes, I feel like a
condemned spirit floating in free space. I observe the people,
how solidly they walk, so rarely alone, with dog or dogs,
boxers with the chronically worried and displeased faces of
bats, waddling along with the incontinent lurch of old men,
but said to be good with children. How that humid gaze does
wander around, scarcely holding back a tear!

Watch them depart in different directions, breast out, seeking Nature's embrace, putting in time until *Kaffee und Kuchen* again. Why, the days revolve around good square meals. How determined they look, so full of, well, *themselves*; they make me sad.

Why is that? Faces from the days gone by, seen in the cold light of morn; where I too see myself as in a broken mirror badly repaired. I've been re-reading old Benn, finding out what I missed years ago, who's who in the graveyards. Do you know that poem which closes: *'Das leere und das gezeichnete Ich?'* Will you return to Nullgrab this fall? Hope you will. There is so much I want to tell you.

Sommerspiele,
Munich, 1972

Nothing upsets Bavarians more than the *Föhn*, a devious Italian wind that slips in over the Alps and whistles through the Brenner, whispering Latin things into German ears. Possibly repeating what *Il Duce* told Count Ciano: that Germans were dangerous because they dreamed collectively.

Be that as it may, when the *Föhn* blows, surgeons lay down their knives and publishers' readers cast aside typescripts, both knowing their judgement to be impaired. Remote objects, such as church spires, draw closer. The good citizens of Munich – where once more I happened to find myself in the Black September of 1972 – like nothing better than to sit for hours on window-seats or out on small balconies, stare into the street below, observe life passing.

In Jakob-Klar-Strasse in Schwabing the retired boxer takes up his position early, and is there all day, fortified by mugs of *Bier* handed out to him by an unseen *Frau*, become just a brawny arm. I was there in the *Schwarzer* September of 1972.

A positively Latin feeling for blueness prevails. *Lividus* bleaching to the delicate washed-out blue of the Bavarian sky over the Englische Garten, in the watery eyes of the citizens, in the flag, on Volksbier labels; it's München blue.

'*Ciao!*' say the better-educated ones on parting; though in the old-style shops the '*Grüss Gotts*' ring out right merrily. Misha Gallé called, then Volker Schlöndorff with his wife Margarete von Trotta for *Tischtennis*.

From Riem Airport into the city the way was festively prepared with huge Olympic flags. My taxi was driven by a woman. I offered Prinzregentenstrasse Fünf as my address, a Freudian slip if ever there was one, and was driven smartly up to Adolf Hitler's old address. I redirected her to a number in Schwabing. The Isar seemed to be flowing the wrong way – a disturbing hallucination.

Once again I began losing my bearings on the wrong side of *Der Friedensengel*, walking my feet off in this city of fine girls and spouting fountains. Greek goddesses with Bavarian thighs, eyes closed against the inevitable, supported on their shoulders heavy pillars pock-marked by bullets fired from afar. The great stone goddesses were protecting the bridges over the Isar, traversed at set intervals by a villainous low-slung black limousine packed with what I assumed to be Italian gangsters, who turned out to be Irish government leaders. *Der Friedensengel* balanced precariously on one foot, hopefully extending a palm branch. Across the plinth an activist had squirted in white aerosol: '*LIEBE DEINE TOTEN!*'

Preparations for the games had intensified throughout summer, with Police Chief Schreiber's men out in waders cleansing the old Isar of a detergent overflow from a factory. On August 28th *Süddeutsche Zeitung* reported that sportsmen and politicians were fascinated (*begeistert*) by an opening ceremony without military undertones. Lord Killanin was in control. Aged Avril Brundage had flown in from the United States. The fire too had come from afar: Greece. Whether this was a good augury or not, few were willing to predict. The American traveller and cynic Theroux would write later that the games were of interest because they showed a World War in pantomime.

But something more disturbing than the *Föhn* (causing double vision) had slipped into Munich with false papers on September 4th when I arrived via Air France from West Berlin (where *Cauldron of Blood* was running at the outpost for occupying troops whose regimental motto had a threatening ring to it: 'Have Guns Will Travel', and be damned to syntax) – Al Fatah. Their target: the Olympic Village. More particularly, Israeli coaches and weightlifters, the heavy innocents stall-fed on milk and T-bone steaks, who were soon to lay down their lives in the German slaughter-house prepared for them.

As bubonic plague, the Black Death, entered Europe as a flea on the body of a rat, so sophisticated international terrorism, late-twentieth-century-style, entered Germany from the Middle East via Riem, in the person of Muhammad Daoud Odeh (code-name Abu Daoud), probably travelling on a forged Iraqi passport. He was to remain there, undetected by Schreiber, throughout the impossible ultimatums – one hostage to be slaughtered every two hours unless 400 or whatever Arab prisoners were released – and the carnage that followed, the self-immolation, the capture of three terrorists at Fürstenfeldbruck military airport.

It was *Föhn* weather, Sharpeville weather, the girls out in summer clothes one day, scarves and coat the next. Police and ambulance sirens never stopped in Leopold-strasse, the dogs barking after the fox has gone. In a mossy fountain, somewhat magnified in the water, small white eggshells broken in halves seemed to tremble. Shabby men were reading discarded newspapers in a public park protected by high hedges. Trams clanged around the steep corner at Max-Planck-Strasse, clinging to the wall. The black limousine was back, now strangely flying the Irish colours on bonnet pennants, with CD registration plates, still traversing old Munich. The Irish Taoiseach Jack Lynch was conferring with Willy Brandt in the country. Buttercups grew along the grass verge on Thomas-Mann-Allee. A woman wearing leather gloves was gathering red berries. Near the Englische Garten two sailors inquired the way to the archery contest, one of them drawing an imaginary bow. Men in shirtsleeves were out. I walked by the embankments, saw the skyline drawn and painted by Klee and Grosz, two brown beauties in bikinis were sunning themselves near the weir where terns were wading; there two Americans had drowned the previous summer. It was a lovely September day, *anno Domini* 1972.

Two workmen in blue denim overalls sat silently at a table on which were arranged some empty beer bottles with the remains of their lunch, under acacia trees buffeted by the wind; a most peaceful scene, one would think. But on Luitpoldstrasse, leading to and from the Olympic Village, the sirens never stopped wailing; it was difficult to distinguish police from ambulances; destination lock-up, hospital or morgue. The call was for law and order; but what is that but disorder with the lid clamped down?

Why was an Irish Embassy car packed with Italian gangsters? Riddles. One handsome terrorist declared that he would have preferred death with his comrades who had blown up victims and themselves with hand-grenades flung into the helicopter. A sombre choral work, then, to be expected in Munich. A style of killing had been set by terrorists who looked more like movie actors than political activists, acted and spoke like them too, in German and broken English, chain-smoking.

The leaves were turning. In shop windows now the signs read '*Hallo Herbst! Du wirst chic*'. The yellow press yelled '*MORDORGIE!*' The headlines screamed '*MORDFEST!*' *The Times* put it more diplomatically, more Britishly: 'STORM GROWS OVER WHAT WENT WRONG AT MUNICH'. *Der Spiegel* of September 11th stated bluntly: '*DAS MASSAKER VON MÜNCHEN!*'

'The XXth Olympic Games resumed yesterday after a 24-hour suspension while Munich mourned the eleven members of the Israeli team who died at the hands of Arab guerrillas.' Mireille Mathieu was driven around the Marathon *Sporthalle*, standing in a white open-top Ford Capri, singing '*Ein Platz an der Sonne für jung und alt*'; while *Papst* Paul VI, not to be outdone, was photographed in Venice, standing precariously upright in what was described as *eine Prunkgondel*, solemnly blessing some Venetian sewage, a clotting of flowers and scum. To the rear of the precarious vessel stood what appeared to be Roman centurians.

The Schwabing flat had been cleaned and the rugs had their colours renewed. Framed on the walls were strange tortured viscerae, possibly human, in monochrome. A single flower, richly red, damask, with streaks of sunflower yellow in its heart, hung in a small blue vase. Red of anther, hush of autumn, tread of panther.

We went swimming in Starnberger See, Erika and Wolfgang and I. Out there in the blue, insane Ludwig had drowned with his physician. The wooded hills rolled away. On Saturday the *Süddeutsche Zeitung* obituary notices faced pages of movie advertising of unrestrained lewdness. Marie Garibaldi was showing her all in *Amore Nudo*. 'MEIN TREUER LEBENSKAMERAD', the obituary notice declared with melancholy certitude. The dead could not cavort with Marie Garibaldi. Hitachi advertised, 'I am you', with Oriental guile. It was time for MacBaren's Golden Blend. It was time for Volksbier. Müller, the man with two left feet, had scored again, and was being ardently embraced by his captain Beckenbauer. *Tip-Kick Fussball* brings competitive fever (*Wettkampfstimmung*) into the home. A modern German family were shown in the throes of 'Tip-Kicking'. Charles Bronson was appearing in *Brutale Stadt*, Jerry Lewis elsewhere, a black detective appeared in *Shaft* ('*Der absolute Super-Krimi!*'). The girls of the DDR ran away with all the track and field events; a splendid example of specialized breeding and expert coaching achieving good results within three decades. An exhibition of early Bavarian folk-art was showing at the Staatliches Museum.

Germans togged out for golf are a sight for sore eyes. They go in for overkill, armed with *Golfschläger*s, but cannot laugh at themselves, unlike the English, who do it tolerantly all the time. Nor can they endure their own Germanic incompetence. A game without visible opponents disturbs; and at golf you are your own opponent, even in matchplay. How they suffer! They *detest* losing. By the eighteenth none are on speaking terms.

I played with the Wittys and their elderly female friend on a woody links in the Bavarian Alps above Chiemsee. The lake itself was invisible below in the haze. I spent most of the round searching for lost golfballs among trees; the lovely Hannelore flushed and peeved, saying 'Shit! Shit!' between clenched teeth.

Back to Munich by train with two well-preserved mountain-hikers, man and wife, in deerstalker and *Loden*s. A relief to be off the *Golfplatz*. (Watch them tearing up the rough, cursing blind. It is a game unsuited to their temperament.) Back in München again, passing *Oktoberfest* tents and stalls.

Prone to a certain kind of spiritual narcosis with which they are afflicted, more so than most races, the Germans must *suffer* themselves. Your average Bavarian is a baleful mixture of sentimentalist and brute. Krüger has his trouser-legs shorted by a Herr von Bismarck, Munich tailor, who asked him on which side he wore his shame.

It sounded grosser in German. Intemperance, fist-fights, puking, in those lovely Ember Days. Stay clean. Tripper and Raptus were on the rampage, Dominguin gored at Bayonne (*carneada* is always the fault of the *torero*). Nature abhors a vacuum. *Neu! Ajax mit der Doppelbleiche.*

Chefpolizist Schreiber negotiated with a terrorist whose head was covered with a woman's stocking. Itchy-fingered *Sturmkommando*s were dressed like frogmen in athletic tracksuits; they watched privily from their hiding-places. *Omnipotenz, Super-Helden!*

The aneroid temperature registered somewhere between '*veränderlich*' and '*Verstörung*', or something between distraction and bewilderment. *Stern* displayed a corn-yellow blonde in the act of unpeeling a corn-yellow T-shirt, her only article of clothing; stamped on her backside were the joined circles of the Olympic symbol, most poshlustily.

Clouds pass over the roofs of Munich, a blue evening falls. The ex-boxer points down into darkening Jakob-Klar-Strasse, amused by something below. There are moments when I am able to look without any effort through the whole of creation (*Schöpfung*), which is nothing more than an immense exhaustion (*Erschöpfung*), wrote stout Thomas Bernhardt.

Gusty *stürmisch* windtossed weather; then a warm sunny day in Munich. The face on the screen, on high hoardings, was out in the streets, the violence let loose. Hands were constantly feeling and touching, groping and tapping. Fingers parted long hair, touched noses, brows, the bearded lips rarely smiled, the looks exchanged were just severe or merely sullen. Hands were never for one moment still, compulsively pulling and picking; plucking at the backs of leather seats, tearing paper, restless, agitated, never still, the eyes restless.

In the capitals of the West the same feature films were released simultaneously. *Little Pig-Man. My Name is Nobady (sic).* 'LIEBE' was sprayed indiscriminately over walls. Amerika Haus was riddled with bullets. The riot squads sat in paddywagons behind wire mesh and bullet-proof glass, parked in backstreets near universities, out of sight, played cards, bided their time. A Judas-grille opened and a baleful eye observed us. In the heated bar the tall lovely unsober teacher Barbara König was swallowing ice-cubes, pulling faces.

Ach ach; *tich-tich*. We cannot stop even if we wanted to, have become voyeurs watching atrocious acts. The lies are without end because the hypotheses are without end. It has become suspect to 'think'; all adults occupy the thrilling realm of moral dilemmas (civic inertia), political drama; *Strassentheater*. Dangerous blindness with a dash of singularity. Angels, for the man who cannot avoid thinking about them, wrote the pessimist Cioran, certainly exist. *So sitzt es mir im Gemüt.*

On the large screens of TV colour sets in the windows of banks the Olympic Games went on, in silence, in triplicate. The high pole-vaulter in the briefest of shorts lifted herself on unseen springs, collapsing in slow motion onto a large bolster. The DDR female athletes were pouring over the hundred-metre hurdles, elegant as bolting deer in a forest fire. From the rapt tormented expression of the long-legged high-jumper, one knew that track records were being broken now in the head. The athletes on the podium were crowned with the bays, gave clench-fisted salutes as their national flag flew on the mast.

In West Berlin at midnight, in the small white flat of a

pregnant beauty, the phone rang, the ringing tone muted. A hidden voice, a Basque voice (not a Berlin accent) said into her ear: '*Es wird noch kommen!*' It would come . . . It still would come. Out in the Olympic Village the twenty-five hostages were still alive. The ultimatum was that one would be killed every two hours, beginning 15 *Uhr* or 3 p.m. Central European Time.

On Kurfürstendamm, advertising an empty cinema, two enormous Sapphic heads regard each other steadfastly with frantic blue-tinged eyeballs, across an illuminated movie façade. Something funny is going on between those two. On high hoardings opposite Marga Schoeller's bookshop the braced bodies of huge nude females proclaim a stressful poshlust, *luxuriante*. A nude female crawls into a tent, pursued by a nude male on all fours. Above the murderous traffic that runs all night, a cut-out of the slain actress Sharon Tate looks over her shoulder at the human clotting below, the sandwichboard-man advertising strip-joints, the Berlin hurdy-gurdy man cranking out an old tune, the prowling beard-stroking hippies, the beads and bangles set out on the wide pavement, like a temporary camp in a jungle clearing. 'PIGS', her murderers had scrawled on the Polanski door; Manson's tribe. Disordered thoughts, *Chaos oder Anarchie* in the here and now. Karl Kraus had defined German girls: 'Long legs, obedience'; not any more.

All strove for a dissipated appearance; many achieved it. Sunglasses were worn indoors, even in ill-lit bars in the depths of winter. Insane seers and mad putative leaders sprang up, were applauded, discussed, shot at, vanished from the scene. Graffiti abounded. The young revolutionaries sprayed aerosol everywhere. '*ANARKI ELLER KAOS!*', as though the terms were not synonymous. The message hardly varied. In the La Rouche district of Paris it ran: '*LIBÉREZ HESS!*'

An underground disco pulses redly: the Mouth of Hell. The pace is set to hedonism, gluttony, the here and now. Frantic with betrayal, two inverts copulate near the Spree in the headlights of a parked car, in a thin rain. (The woodcock, wily bird, is said to dress its own wounds. Partridges sleep with one eye open. The Chinese, more observant than most, maintain that the rat changes into a quail, the quail into an oriole. The female muskrat, as everybody knows, is the mother of the entire human race. Unless I am thinking of the Eskimos' Sedna. Muskrats are barren when in captivity; if they breed, they devour their young. A young Munich veterinario blamed stress induced by crowded conditions; or, more likely, the fact of being under constant observation by humans.)

In West Berlin (population 2.2 million souls) every second citizen is over forty years; more than twenty-five per cent over sixty-five. Thirty-nine thousand die each year, with thirteen thousand more dying than are being born; every third citizen owns a dog.

Frau Meinhardt likes to curry-comb her two Airedales on the balcony, and curly orange hair floated into our morning coffee. She drove to Malta in a green sports car, a nice change of air for the nervous bitches, mother Anya and whelp, a classical illusion. There was no shade in Malta, it was bad for the dogs.

She, the war-widow, never referred to her late husband; the fine house in Nikolassee was all that remained of that lost life. The old heart of the city was dead – Unter den Linden. She owned a house in Wiesbaden, let out the Berlin property; demonstrated how to work the vacuum cleaner, a *Walküre* model, adding on tubular parts and a rigid snout. When devouring dirt the bag swelled, set up a strident whine, began snarling, all snout and stomach. A true German machine.

Tall beauties paraded on Kurfürstendamm, displaying themselves in tight jeans, that was the accepted uniform of chic. The boutiques advertised a worn but not yet threadbare look, that was the fashion. Their manner implied: 'We belong to the streets'; and, by analogy – false – 'The streets belong to us'. *Strassentheater*.

Freedom marches followed protest marches, the squatters occupying empty buildings. They were untouchable,

101

in a way. They, too, were in the dream, living the dream. They occupied the streets, seemingly at home there, some living a hand-to-mouth existence, squatting before lines of trinkets, metalwork. Wearing sandals like gurus and holy men, or going about barefoot; footloose as Rastafarians, Reb stragglers from the American Civil War, fuzzi-wuzzies from Abyssinia, Tibetan monks with shaven polls; the females were even more lightly dressed, as though in perpetual summer (*'La naturale temperature des femmes,'* quoth Amyot in a soft aside, *'est fort humide'*), their extremists more dangerous than the males. In West Berlin the Black Cells, the Anarchists, went among the passive resisters like hyenas among zebra.

Insistence on the unique and particular had spawned the microbe Duplication. The face on the screen was in the street. The violence there was let loose here, in the open, the dream gone mad. They were actors and actresses playing bit-parts in a continuing series. The face on the hoardings walked the streets. The Individual as such was disappearing, had disappeared; only remained, in a disordered milieu grown ever grubbier, more dangerous. The world's capitals had become *pissoirs*.

On fine summer evenings, in Málaga and Athens, Copenhagen and Munich, long cinema queues waited to watch a violent surrogate existence run on huge screens, the sound monstrously distorted. 'To learn is to have something done to one.' Why bother about Bach if a saxophone gives you an idea of eternity? Their own life had ceased to interest them. Huge hoardings displayed a Red Indian brave naked from the waist up, advertising a brand of shampoo. Rock cellars throbbed, their lurid entrances leading down into an inflamed red throat. *Schlagermusik*.

Hungarian camomile, asafoetida gum, aeroplane grease, cola nuts, Syrian rue, fly agaric, horsetail, skullcap, yohimbine, these were popular. In Absurdia the poor drank the urine of the high rich. Informed heads, *Tagträumer*, trippers, might tell of the so-called Jackson Illusion Pepper, with a hole at one end and a cigarette at the other through which the entire contraption might be smoked to provide colourful and elaborate hallucinations.

Road-hippies on endless round trips sold their blood in Kuwait; took overdoses, observed the 'way-out' regions inhabited by the teeming poor of the miserable Third World. Lost ones blew their brains out. A huge organ was playing at noon in a department store heavy with controlled artificial air. Shoppers, passive as fish, stunned by pumped *Musik*, ascend and descend by escalators. Overpriced commodities were sold by ingenious advertising campaigns, an all-out 'psychological' war not on want but on plenty. Everything was oversold, overheated; fraternity too had become a Hell. The cities were splitting up from within, supermarts and car parks replacing cathedrals and concert halls. On fine summer evenings the long cinema queues waited silently in the north. To flee the world and dream, the past, was their intent; a sourceless craving now externalized, brought close. For them it would always be *Sperrmüll-Tag*: Throwing-Out Day.

Alcoholic professors taught their own version of history. The students were apprehensive to leave the campus. In the surrounding woods maniacs prowled all night, whistling. The young kept to their dormitories, debated much on their 'development', always making schemes. Schedules were drawn up, abandoned. Believing that life goes in steps, exclusively concerned with drugs of one sort or another, hard politics, India-Buddha teachings, claptrap about 'freedom'. Their future was grim. But the protestors went marching anyway. They were lost in the dream. Their own parents were the irrecoverable Past.

On which side do you wear your shame?

Faina Melnik in athletic hotpants was displaying the Popo look, said to have been imported from Japan. The discus was thrown an unlikely distance by an unlikely looking female. The huge Israeli weightlifters were all dead, blown to kingdom come. The games had gone on. The so-called Day of Mourning had been nothing less than hypocrisy; too much money was invested, too many interests involved; national honour had been at stake. The word had come down that the terrorists were not to leave German soil with their victims. Too much was at stake. The terrorists themselves had shown less hypocrisy; they were not interested in deals or (even) human life. *Rheinischer Merkur* had its *'Mordorgie'*. 'Aroused Prussia' was a lard factory. A *mortadella* mincing machine.

'RUSS MAY BEEF UP NAVY IN MED', spoke out the *New York Herald Tribune*. 'BODIES OF SLAIN ATHLETES REACH LODZ, FLOWN FROM MUNICH' (American speaking). Lodz Airport, soon to receive its own baptism of fire from Japanese *kamikaze* terrorists. *Falsche Spekulation der Luftpiraten!* At the Staatliches Museum an exhibition of early Bavarian folk-art was on display. Art, 'progress' (towards what?) comes from weaponry, not from the kitchen. The arms of the foot-soldiers, peasant conscripts, were no different in kind from their primitive work-tools. Art and progress were displayed in the finely decorated swords and pistols of their mounted officers.

Der Bomber (Müller) scores again.

In the Neue Nationalgalerie in West Berlin hang two paintings commemorating the Student Uprising of '68 in Paris; Renato Guttuso's *Studentenumzug mit Fahnen* and *Barrikaden in Paris*. To the sad cliché of the street barricade, the hero with flag unfurled, the brave corpses, must now be added the Faceless Terrorist.

Leni Riefenstahl's extraordinary *Fest der Völker* was showing at the Arri (8 *Woche*). The XIth Olympiad at Berlin in 1936. In the old recruiting documentary the plumes of smoke rising densely black around the Imperial Eagle might have come from Hell itself. Wagner shows me a world I am not sure I would wish to enter. Stout Hermann Goering, the cocaine addict, shaken with helpless laughter; Hitler leaning forward, rubbing together his cold political hands. Hess, his putative son, all eye-socket and jaw, watched Jesse Owens, assuredly no Aryan, run away with all the track events. A cinema full of war-widows watched in an uncanny silence. What was one to make of the spider in the web, before the credits rolled, and the scalped athletes running naked around a Berlin lake, through early morning mist? No symbols where none intended.

Misha Gallé had been permitted an interview when Leni Riefenstahl, still a handsome woman, had learnt that *her* father had been a Nazi judge. She told Misha Gallé that Herr Hitler had been a good man led astray by 'bad companions'(!). The homosexual Röhm? The war-widows dispersing silently from the Arri, set their mouths in grim lines and, separated for *Kaffee und Kuchen*, were offering no comments.

Two months later a Lufthansa flight into Munich was hijacked and the three terrorists sprung from three high-security prisons sixty miles apart. When interviewed, they chain-smoked, spoke in broken English and were reported to be of 'terrifying' niceness. They had the rugged good looks of movie actors and justified their actions at length; somewhere in the world ravishing girls awaited their return.

In February 1973, Abu Daoud, now passing himself off as a Saudi sheik, was arrested in central Amman by a Jordanian security patrol. His 'wife' was a fifteen-year-old girl carrying a handgun and ammunition clips, which, on being arrested, she dropped. 'Abu Daoud's' forged passport showed him to be the father of six children. His own father worked in Jerusalem as a labourer for the Israeli City Council.

September 16th had been the last day of the XXth Olympiad. All the shops were closed and the Schwabing streets deserted, a dead day. Misha Gallé played *Tischtennis* with Wolfgang. On the huge Olympic board the last farewells: 'AVRIL BRANDAGE' (*sic*) for all the world to see. Twenty *Grad* of *Bodenfrost* on September 28th. *Das Ende der Saison.*

Meanwhile the super-rat, immune to all poisons, had arrived in Rio. Six dead. Abu Daoud, where are you now?

Autumn in Cómpeta

1976

The natives of these parts have a pithy saying to the effect that 'nothing dead lasts long'. Headgear, as various as the owners, is worn as if hats had just been invented, clamped or stitched to the head and removed most reluctantly, the abstracted hand passed over the scorched scalp and head-gear replaced with an anguished expression as if something long-pondered had at last been resolved. Then air is expelled from the mouth – 'Ouff!', a husky fifenote. The hats might be narrow-brim, well-worn straw, sweated-into grey Homburg, elegant Anthony Eden, dusty black beret with a little knob at the crown. Their gossiping is liberally enlivened with '*¡Cojónes!*', the male term for emergent life.

Insects rise; all is calm; a breeze blows from the right hand, the olive trees shiver, exposing their silvery under-sides. Now a mule is led past by an old man with head lowered, a small dog standing on the saddle like a circus act. I hear the robin in the valley, a repeated series of high fidgety twitterings.

The wind whines in the fence about the ugly new barracks-like edifice of red brick. To the rear of this awkward structure, as you go by San Antonio, I heard the wind whine and took it to be the demented droning of hens shut up for the night and rallying themselves for sleep on their perch. But it was only five o'clock on a late October afternoon, far too early for fowl to be shut up. The wind went gustily as a vibraphone through the wire fence as I passed down into the valley full of birds.

Below the finest little mosque in all Christendom, con-verted centuries ago into a Catholic church and now a chapel of rest for corpses from Canillas *en route* to the *cementerio*, stood an ugly new factory for the manufacture of sanitary towels or disposable knickers, which afforded labour to the local girls.

I had heard the plangent sound of a guitar near the round threshing-stone where they still worked the grain in the old way, throwing it into the air to winnow it. Along the road there the *novios* conducted their courtship in the old style, walking out together as in Straffan and Naas and Clane in the summers of long ago, on the by-roads free of motorized traffic. It reminded me of a past which now hardly seems to belong to me, this by-road slow-linking courtship, and the drone of hens, a valley of birds, perpetual summer. Mere tokens, signs of oncoming senility and nothing more. Token symptoms of insanity making a strong effort to be reasonable. Sufficient to say that hereabouts all nature is in gentle riot.

Coming from a day of walking in the hills I had heard a male voice singing from a high place and thought I saw a figure working on the mosque but when I came below the mosque the singing human figure had become part of the electrical installation. There, on the other side where the swallows fly below the path, the land seems to induce song. Finding themselves on high places the men have an urge to sing and in those hours when the light is going fast their songs most resemble the evening prayer-songs of their old conquerors calling out of their minarets, all turned to the east. As sometimes too, when very drunk, the involuntary cries are wrung from them. A tilted condition suited to Canillas and Competa, hill villages put together at angles of forty-five degrees, and thus a uniquely tilted drunkenness, and they call out in great distress, this double syllable of anguish, a cry wrung from the mouths of men who should not drink at all, let alone drink to excess, and ulcers at fifty. Again the distressed cry from the mouths of their conquerors who in the eight long centuries of occupation had kept their own religion and become assimilated into España, particularly in the province closest to their own land and most resembling it. Become in fact another race. Not of España but a mixture of the two races, become a third mixed race called *los Moros*. Two great trading races come to live as one, when the time for trading for both had ended.

¡AAAAaaaiii! ¡¡AAAaaaaiiiiie!!', the tortured drunk cries out from the high bedroom window, just a slit in the outer wall, presumably holding onto the bed-rail within, his eyes closed. How mortally ashamed of myself am I! How mortified that I am I, and so drunken in Cómpeta!

The ones who did not drink stayed on to build aqueducts for the dry impoverished land and by an ingenious system of ways and means brought water and vegetation into dried-out valleys and even raised up their own dreamlike architecture within the conquered towns and cities, a nomad dream of palms and palaces and cool secret places fit for rendezvous. But above all watercourses and fountains, the most persistent nomad dream: flowing water.

And the other, the other half, the body of the land that nothing could transform, and the people on it whom no conqueror could change, no matter how long the conquest? It and they sank into poverty together, into a prolonged dream out of which not even General Franco himself could wake them, but rather plunged them deeper, further from their own nature.

Near the old Arab cemetery – as strange as an English cemetery in India, even to long-dead English names on gravestones – Trull and the semi-demented painter and whilom remittance man Carsten had observed three silent dark citizens, in that port of pickpockets, drug-pushers, perverts and outstretched palms. Observed them seated side by side on a public bench, swaying gently this way and then that as the wind turned; the breeze passed through their beards again, they turned with it, saying nothing but smiling to themselves, hooded in their desert clothes. They smiled because they felt *other than themselves*, part of the breeze that blew through the palm trees, part of another

111

race. They were curious to be alive, smiling to themselves as they swayed on the bench near or in the cemetery there.

Conrad wrote that curiosity is one of the forms of self-revelation. Duplication of vision: I see an image with multiple forms in the light, trembling in the glare of Arab day. On yet another occasion, not unfree of incident, Trull and I had spent a day in Tangier. He limping around with an ingrowing toenail and far from cordial. We were pestered by pickpockets and an itinerant trader of woollen caps whom we could not shake off. Wherever we went he was sure to be there before us, or just coming in the door after us, or walking by outside and hailing us, a fellow who claimed to be Charlie Chaplin. The woollen caps were made in the interior.

After being silently molested on the sea-front by a pickpocket we took a meal among Berbers in a sort of lean-to in the main square. An ancient Berber leaning across was civil enough to inform the crusty Trull that salt was bad for him. Or so we understood from his dumbshow and grimaces. Trull poured out a liberal handful into his soup and over his meat, and bending down applied himself to his meal, causing the ancient Berber to withdraw into his djellaba in the most frosty manner imaginable.

We found a bar with wide windows overlooking the passing parade and ordered vodka and fresh orange juice. The drinks well iced were hardly set before us than in came Charlie Chaplin, delighted to see us again, calling out 'Tchollie! Tchollie!'

I saw nothing of Chaplin in him, looking for the tramp. But presently, talking to another customer, he drew out a piece of material, cocked his head, sketched a gesture, and there stood the stout white-haired rubicund father of half a dozen children, the Chaplin of *Limelight* with the old talent gone. Enough of Tangier. We flew back, were delayed, ran up a huge drinks bill on Iberia. I feared for my life with a mad Moorish taxi driver, then a low fellow who drove like one possessed from the airport to the town, its lights shuddering in the distance.

But now I am walking in the valley, or sitting on the bridge, smoking a Goya, where the road bends by the Mass Path there. Rounding a corner I came upon a local youth up to his chest in what appeared to be a grave, and still digging. His transistor played Irish traditional music, strange to hear there, and I was back again on Camus Bay in a little cemetery by the crooked seashore and it was raining as usual. Or was I with the countess in a miserable bar overlooking a seaweed factory and a drenched fish-dock with parked cars and from the radio behind the bar a female voice sang soothingly, 'I'd love to see old Ireland free once more.' And then a rendering of 'The Wexford Men of '98'. And then the name of the bar came back to me: Kilkieran's on a bay of the same name.

Now I saw with failing eyesight what I took to be a goat-herd effortlessly transforming himself into several divided beings. The intent here was in no way clear to me. I was sitting on one of those blocks of cemented brick that guard the bend, then I saw him above me, over the road, on a ridge in the company of half a dozen goats, a roan ram and buff ewes to be pedantic. He seemed to be addressing them. Sounds carry far in that acoustic valley. I heard the rough voice going on amiably, confidentially. They talk to dogs here, and to the earth, so why not to goats. Perhaps he was whiling away the time telling them the old stories?

The oldest and best stories in the world, the ones that do not change. Of the snakes that venture down from the mountains in hot weather and swim in the aqueducts or even crawl into the gardens by the sea to drape themselves in the oleander. Or even venture into the house, out of curiosity, or for the cool, and drape themselves around the toilet seat, for coolness that takes some beating. And very unsettling for the person at stool or for a woman looking down at what are supposed to be water-pipes and sees a snake, as has indeed happened to me. Or of the one who gets into a lady's handbag.

Or tales of the foxes who steal the grapes and rob from

the *basuras*, the trash barrels, hunting not singly but in groups. And the meaning of their mournful nocturnal cries. Or, nearer home, of the known potency of Cómpeta wine, stored in great barrels in cool places. To my way of thinking a cross between bad sherry and worse Montilla, and certain death to the liver when not taken in moderation, which is the way it is generally taken. Or of strong coffee with goat's-milk laced with Cognac, good on cold nights. Or taken with *churros*. Better still on cold mornings, with a shot of anise, a shock to the system, a pecker-up, a stirrer of the blood sluggish at that hour. All these without exception good things.

Or of the taste of *callos*, which we call tripe, or *pulpo*, which is octopus with its eight suckered arms around the mouth. Or of all the good things that dwell in the sea. And of the force of *cerdo* (pork), for pig is everywhere and in everything, their death-shrieks heard one night of every week. So tenacious of a life that never seemed so good, now that it is ending. *Adíos* to the carefree hours in the piggery, always good. *Cerdo* cooked with the *vino terreno* and teeth of *ajo* (garlic), for garlic certainly goes with everything.

And the goats, who had certainly heard these stories before, and many times, or stories very like them – being spared only the stories of the pungency of *cabra* itself, good as a main dish, fine as a cheese, excellent fine as *tapas*, titbits given free in bars with orders of drink – stories of slaughtered kids, not to put too fine a point upon it. Good as milk, which is said to inhibit potency. But this is surely incorrect, for the milk in the Bar Perico near the church was always goat's-milk, and Luis Perico himself was the father of eleven sons and daughters.

The same stories told in exactly the same words, the blurred dreamlike words of the old story, for any deviation would be wrong. The same stories told over and over. And told to the goats before them, back to the great dreamlike herds of their forebears on the plains, in the time of the black and blue men brought over by General Franco to put the fear of God into the whole province. Men with black and blue faces and cut-throat propensities, in the endless centuries of the occupation. And before that in the time of the seagoing Phoenicians, who had brought rabbits into Andalucía and tin to Málaga.

It was doubtless with yarns like these that the herdsman was boring the udders off the ewes. Or with others as similar or as long-winded, a pleasant way of passing the time. Or perhaps again stories of the lewdness of all foreign women, whose morals were by definition habitually loose. When carnal tendencies take hold of them then Satan himself must be allowed to work his way. Or of the lustful ways of abbesses, having their way with abbots and bishops, gardeners too, in the cool privacy of the cells, lips if not anus gleaming with glycerine and eyes ablaze with unquenchable lust. Or of all the good growing things of the earth, never limp, no good in bed but splendid up against a wall.

I hear the nanny-goats sniggering in the private evasive way by which these contemplative beasts express their not so dumb amusement, the ram hee-heeing away like old Cornok himself into its shaggy beard.

Now the scraggy leaves of the cane plantation fidget in the breeze as it pours through their rows. Depressed as old coats on hangers stand the stems, turning up their curled leaves. The sugar bushes, some call them.

A small cloud appears over the ridge, brief as a puff of smoke from a steam-engine, appearing in the evening of this cloudless blue day. On the path below, the trampled form of a frog with outstretched arms is imprinted in the dust, with a few spent cartridges for company. The hunting season has started and the guns are going in the hills. Then the cloud has evaporated and the herdsman appears to be now addressing himself to an unseen friend, for I seem to hear other rough tones answering. The goats cavort on the slopes, enjoy the play of air, as the evening breeze comes up the steep narrow valley full of so many varieties of birds.

Now again all is calm on the slope, the human voices silent. The tattered appendages droop and rustle, as if despised, aware of their poverty, just old useless coats, as the wind, gathering force, rushes through them, setting them all to fidgeting and trembling. And the two owls who have been calling to each other have settled on one branch on a tree over the *barranca*. In two hours it will be dark. Are they even owls? Their sharp cries octaves above hooting.

It's a boy whom the herdsman addresses, perhaps his grandson. The goats are browsing, the herdsman wrapped in his mantle, the boy staring down at the road where nothing moves, least of all me.

And presently the boy has disappeared and the herdsman is standing hurling stones and abuse at his flock who scatter, some escaping to higher ledges and others jumping down. I hear the rough voice choking. But in a little while they come together again and he seems to be frolicking with them.

Now seated, a long confabulation ensues between the one seated on a rock and another unseen one. I hear distinctly '*Dos cognac*'. But now the herdsman addresses himself only to a low silent form, perhaps not even human . . .

When attempting the language it is foolish to speak slowly or attempt clear articulation, for that way will get you nowhere. First the gutturals must be mastered, no easy job, since the language abounds in gutturals. As you move higher into the hills it becomes harder to follow, closer to true Arab, the words running together. In the north they speak another language: Catalán. Another race altogether, stolid, unimaginative, hard-working; a people whose chief gifts to España have been bankers and industrialists, latterly terrorists in the cause of independence. Their language is inherited from the Stone Age, now slowly dying out because unsuited to modern times, and so difficult that no one can learn it.

With Cómpeta *español* a general picture is preferable; the submerged constructions surfacing and sending the rest out towards what may not be total comprehension but at least partial and, moreover, sounding as though delivered in an idiom generally acceptable in the village. A fish held in the palm of the hand first thing in the morning is thought to bring luck.

To them, and more so to their children's ears, English sounds a feeble and indeed ridiculous tongue, a trance-speech of caste. '*Weeeshywashy!*', the children call out in mockery on hearing English spoken.

The married women retire at sunset and are up at cockcrow. They laugh a lot, shrug their shoulders and laugh off misfortune. All are watchful observers, the habit deepening with age, particularly among the males, who seem to be observing themselves rather than you, attentive to some inner process, their cane chairs tilted against the wall of the church or arranged in a half-circle outside the Mirror Bar: the Old Hats, Trull calls them, being a bit of an old hat himself. They have a complicated expression for these long murmurous discussions, their retelling of the day's events, for which the synonym might be the-last-shout-on-the-stairs. Their language well reflects the charming and uncomplicated nature of the people themselves. God's name is in everything they say, as in Connemara or Bavaria. Hissed imprecations are a sign of exasperated sensibility and nothing more. They are past masters of the contrapuntal serpent hiss. Abstract thought is unknown to them and when they hear it attempted they become embarrassed. Hence perhaps the need for nights of loud convivial shouting in the bars, with which the village is liberally supplied, after a day spent labouring on the land. Overcoats are never worn, not even in the severest winters, but umbrellas carried.

Empty the head of preconceived notions and fill the mouth full of syllables and then spew them out with little or no regard for accuracy or even sense. In this you will gain a reputation for speaking their mountain lingo 'very well', even though no single word has been understood. It is the sounds that matter and the intent behind the sounds, generally hammered home with the hand, a vein in the forehead throbbing. While no strangers to the ecstatic vision, up there at 550 metres, it's considered the height of bad manners to refer to this. The word for savings bank is identical to the word for coffin. They are a happy people.

The Dogs of Cómpeta

1977

The dogs of Competa, the most silent breed in the world, give tongue loud and aggrieved when kicked, as if no dog had ever been kicked in Cómpeta before. But is it not rather their proud and contentious spirits that have been abused and not their canine nature, considering that they hardly behave as dogs at all? The ones that guard the flocks do not behave as one would expect, protecting the wings and rounding up strays, but slink along with vacillating tread more like soldiers behind gun-carriages at state funerals than dogs herding goats. On the skyline, almost home, posed in heraldic style, dexter paw raised, they scarcely resemble dogs; and in this I believe they imitate the leading goat, a bearded ram with a tangled span of horns, the progenitive parts protected in a leather truss; becoming more and more hesitant as they near home, pushing forward only to stop, hesitating, as if uncertain of their whereabouts, or their welcome.

Stray sheep with long unclipped tails move among the main goat-herds, the frisky half-grown lambs steal the ewes' milk on the sly; among them also pigs, self-sufficient and busy as only dirty pigs can be.

Dried skins of snakes are prized as treatment for mules with the colic. To *think* of a fox (*zorra*) is considered to be an unlucky omen. The herdsmen, powerful sling-shots, carry furled black umbrellas when foul weather threatens and, sometimes, transistor sets.

The voices of the males are rough. As boys they had perhaps shouted to each other overmuch in the hills, argued the toss too heatedly in the blaring bars, smoked too much strong black tobacco (Goya), drank too deeply of the potent local wine, orange-hued and midway to being sherry, that produces ulcers.

The young males cluster together and jeer but keep to themselves, congregating above the plaza meeting-place and the promenade called *paseo*, sheltered by plane trees, from where on a clear day it is possible to see the Dark Continent in the form of the Atlas Mountains, the oldest in the world.

The women's voices are most raucous in the morning, pulling one (by the roots) out of the deepest slumbers, as the pitch of their excitement rises, their fury one might think, if you did not know them; so that surely blows must follow. But no, the early arguments end in high-pitched screeches and good-natured morning banter. They are both simple and baffling.

Stout Carmela, mother of two hairy sons, loudest and merriest of all, and old childless Fernanda with the blind spectacles and a twisted knee, her husband dead of cancer, lead the screeching.

Women beyond child-bearing have registers of the highest pitch, as if in a state of perpetual wonder and bewilderment, *permanently* surprised. The younger women, particularly the girls waiting for marriageable males, are quiet and rather withdrawn, speaking hardly at all; the formally engaged ones retreat even further into themselves, possibly obsessed with trousseaus. Some head of cattle, a rough breed, are now kept and can be heard bellowing in the ravine near the kohl-burner's cave.

Send us canorous! Here even the mountain streams are noisier than elsewhere.

Fire (*fuego*) has a different meaning, another secret power. I saw a little girl dancing in a fire. At the all-night kohl-burning, women with their menses must keep away. The log on the open hearth is embraced by arms of fire, split in twain by fire. The tree struck by lightning ignites in the storm at night, in torrential rain, burns away an area to the dimensions of a football pitch, watched from the high road as it happened, seen some days later, a burnt-out area among evergreens.

They have no nightcarts or refuse collections as such, but with little or no regard for hygiene, all the refuse and filth of the place is flung into two narrow gorges situated at each end of the uptilted village. *Caca* is 'shit' with all that it implies, though '*¡Nueva caca!*' (with a brandishing of the right fist and a rolling upward of the eyes) is regarded as a friendly greeting. (The refuse piles in the ravines, with dead or dying animals, might be regarded as their version of our professional thieves, soiling unspeakably the collected linen of a robbed house, 'posting a sentry').

They have Evil Eyes painted on the bottoms of their chamber-pots.

They are very superstitious, believe in ghosts ('the Other Ones'); carry heavy old-fashioned black umbrellas as people unaccustomed to rain, although it rains torrentially through January and even February. The postman, a hopeless drunkard in green gumboots, is seen disappearing into the mulemen's bar and that's the end of the postal delivery for the day. His customary greeting to me: '*¡Hoy nada!*' ('Today nothing!'). The drunken barber brandishing a cut-throat razor leaves a customer profusely bleeding, only shrugs his shoulders. *¡Nada!* again: hypnotic stasis.

It is close to impossible to embarrass or get a rise out of them, though it can be done. When overcome by embarrassment (but on your account), and really put out, they show it by absenting themselves, slowly averting the head and lowering the eyes, with all the monumental dignity of dumb brutes. It may rankle for a while and will then be overlooked and forgotten in as far as such breaches of manners can be forgotten. In the quiet end-of-season time, given over to flies and hunters out after *perdigón* (a sort of partridge), the same hunters seldom sober by evening, the old men play a game like dominoes in the small main plaza, and card-games everywhere, or rather one single game, a game without numerals.

Some days ago an old man of eighty years died when

crushed by a backing truck and pinned against the wall of the raisin factory. All his life had been spent in that vicinity near the dump and there too he had died, pressed in against the sunny wall where he had liked to take the air. Some years before, after betting on a single lottery number all his life, he was called away to sick relatives and gave up his number to an unmarried officer of the Guardian Civil, whereupon his number came up and the delighted bachelor received one million pesetas. The old man gave up buying lottery tickets. In the manner of his going, the village expressed neither sorrow for the one nor censure for the other (a youth who had no licence), believing that chance prevailed to a great extent and one could be sure of nothing, except that one would die one day. *Nada*. It was a word often on the lips of the women; no doubt the main tenet in a daunting philosophy that kept them all in such boisterous fettle.

How soon the voices cease and evening silence falls! Among the group on the wall below, waiting for their evening meal, the stories become bolder as darkness comes on, and it falls suddenly here. Two glasses full, two empty, two glasses refilled here on the terrace; below they drink nothing. Now comes the turn of the planet Venus. '*¿Maria, Maria, que dice?*' ('Marie, Marie, what are you saying?') '*¡Mírame, Maria!*' ('Look at me, Marie!'). Soon they retire and the wall is empty. Darkness falls on Competa. Even the cuckoo in the olive tree behind the house falls silent. Do cuckoos call at night? Always silent at night. A curious lone bird, when one calls, is it to another, or for themselves alone that they call out with the strangest of all bird-calls, in these hills at least, odder than the fig pickers that whirr in the air in October. Messiaen heard an unknown bird calling in Persia, in the evening, and put it into his hymn-work as the voice of God, not thunder but a voice close to silence, and therefore nearer to God, one can safely assume. The silence that now on the terrace falls, and on Competa below, is an intimation of the great silence that

124

will one day descend and never lift again. The globe and its wretched burden of history was only a dream, a bad dream only in God's head, on an off-day long past, now whirled into space, nothingness.

It is fine weather now, the sun very hot during the days and cool in the evening. You can see the currents in the sea some thirty kilometers below us, down the valley beyond the hill-villages (*pueblos*) called El Clot (where they cast stones at strangers), Ab Oxú (ill-lit and dry all summer) and Nulles (haunt of half-wits who throw stones at each other), and the sun goes down very fiery. Getting dark earlier, the two buses coming home with their lights on, ascending all the time, around more than two hundred bends.

The colours of our autumn sky change all the time, minute by minute. The sun goes down and a breeze starts up, the light goes out of the sky, the mountains darken, the *gorriones* (a type of sparrow) end their chittering and depart, leaving droppings like small burnt worms on the terrace. Then the evening ritual of the goats going by, heraldic beasts leading, the main herd anxiously emitting dry farts, knowing home is near. That's how it is in Cómpeta.

Ronda Gorge &
Other Precipices

1979–80

Sex magazines attest to contemporary glut; clipped to the kiosks the toothy photomodels expose a good deal more than their gums. The ancient mossy trees are still in old disarray near the dry riverbed where the last public garotting took place in Málaga. An empty taxi careers past with its indicator raised: '*OCUPADO*'.

The passing of the Generalissimo has seen Spain pass, rather awkwardly (there is no other way), into the latter part of the twentieth century, with strikes, pornography and terrorism. Porno movies feature the Fallen Abbess, Anne Heywood, she also features in *Buena Suerte, Miss Wyckoff* (dir. Marvin Chomsky). Charl Ton Heston (*sic*) bares his teeth manfully in *El Desesperado* at the Zaybe. In an alley on an old wall near a dusty door is painted '*TOD DEN JUDEN*', in a street only fit for pogroms. There is a place for everything, even misfortune, in the Capital of Sorrow.

The very ancient port of Málaga stands for the past; here nothing essential ever changes. Pigs' blood flows into the gutter by the market. Time passes slowly at Portillo, in the shadowy bar Antigua Casa de Guardia (*fundada en* 1840). Black-clothed widows of Spain walk about in their day of perpetual mourning. Bulky men in grey uniforms convey packages to and from Banco de Bilbao, veritable *postillons d'amour*. In the woodsmelling wine-bars stout men in braces are taking their first drink of Muscatel; '20' is chalked again and again on the knife-scarred counter, 20 pesetas for a shot of Dulce. Everywhere I hear that sad-sounding ordinary word: *siempre*. Around the *mercado* by night there's a dreadful smell of old prick. Málaga is full of fruit. *¡Admisión del Rector!* Athens and Málaga are oily cities.

Delicate touchers of cash-registers and balancers of scales; something fresh and fishy is being weighed judiciously. And always the talk of money, *'dinero'* in the mouths of the pasty-faced Latin men – *'¡millónes!'*. King Carlos himself looks permanently constipated on the stamps. Men are blowing their noses gustily into clean linen handkerchiefs, while having their shoes polished. Market women squat on the steps by the bus terminus for Nerja, offering Scotch whisky and French cheese. Calle Córdoba smells, as always, of open drains, dissipation, mournful numbers: an abattoir stench in the streets of pickpockets, male prostitutes. Watch-sellers lie in wait near Portillo, a coach is pulling out for Cadiz. But little by little the pleasing things are going: Hotel Cataluña closed, the Café Español reduced by half. *Cine* hoardings are explicitly horrifying; a naked girl bound to a stake is fearfully impaled, a wooden dagger protruding from a mouth pumping blood, watched by bushmen or cannibals who crouch watchfully near by. Some artist has rendered a pair of convulsively clasped hands, naked as fornicating nudes.

Andalucía, Talmudic as anything alive, is made up of contradictions: *cine* advertising become inverted Catholic iconography *outré* as ever (the Fallen Abbess); blood still flows. While a fat fellow with sunken breasts in a Jaeger jersey stands idle in the doorway of Viajes Marland, not expecting much in the way of trade. It's going to be another hot day in Málaga.

After dark in the Café Español nine ladies arrive carrying Menefis plastic shopping-bags, dressed in moleskins, with one fox-fur; rather Germanic in mien, grim of mouth, with blue eyeshadow. Draping the furs over the backs of their chairs they order Coca-Cola and Cognac. An old-style waiter (Wicklow Hotel, Dublin, *circa* 1946) places a bottle of Cruzcampo at a judicious remove between a nervous young couple, having removed the cap with a wristy one-handed pass, looking elsewhere: a polished gesture of exquisite tact.

The grim-mouthed Ingebabies are now joined by three

others dressed in more expensive woollen jackets, which they throw over the backs of their chairs. Is it a Consciousness-raising session at coffee-break or Málaga wives out on the town?

Cat-fur is worn aggressively by the gum-chewing transvestite whores at the Bar Sol y Sombra near the market. Vermilion lipstick goes ill with hair dyed off-yellow, saffron wigs, heavy make-up, stiletto heels and deep bass voices. They adjust false bosoms, study the effect in the mirror, eyes flash like Semiramis, ignoring the snickering of the young male barmen. Traffic is heavy to and from the *Señoras*. None of them are being picked up – transvestite whores wild in appearance as pro footballers at a drag party.

Are the blind lottery-sellers really sightless, or have they induced blindness upon themselves by an act of will? They circulate about the cathedral, tapping with their white canes. There's much to be seen in Málaga; a strong sense of *déja vu* permeates it; shoe shops for spastics, religious candles for funerals, china cats stare from shop windows; within, candelabras, dire reproductions of landscapes; casseroles and glassware, dinner-plates in opened crates of wrapping stuff. A fellow is artfully arranging a large fish on a slab. Smell of drains and dust; English faces scorched by the winter sun, a last opportunity to swagger a bit.

In the hotel bar above the Alcazaba overlooking the harbour and the bullring, von Stroheim, bald as a coot, riding-crop under one arm, sporting spurs, is throwing back double whiskies.

A pale-faced barman at La Campana wine-bar is deeply immersed in a pornographic magazine printed in Madrid. The evening trade is drinking Seco Montes, P. Ximen, Agte, Seco Añejo and Málaga Dulce tapped from the large barrels ranged behind. The *servicio* is as old as all human ills; a dank place with water dripping from above. Málaga always meant the past. Snails are in. Service in the stationery shop is slow even by Andalusian standards; an unseen transistor plays 'Roll Out The Barrel' in a muted way. Girls in school uniforms, with hockey sticks, pass by. A powerful hose is played over a path to keep the dust down. The city never changes. A bird sings in a cage. Sallow-complexioned businessmen are ordering *sombras* with *churros* in what is left of the Café Español. The Bar Baleares has become yet another shoe shop. Málaga was obsessed by Yo-Yos. Victoria draught beer hard to come by.

Small sailors are propositioning the *chicas* who parade in pairs, giggling; their long hair freshly washed. They are all a-titter; the attentive tars getting nowhere. A collection for the Asociación Protectora Malagueña de Subnormales. Landaus drawn by carriage-horses in foolish hats proceed half asleep down Travesía Pintor Nogales, carrying tourists. Saigon has fallen, the English pound is dropping, American public opinion rising.

'*TYRANNIQUE OU TROP CONCILIANTE?*', cry the kiosks. 'SAIGON PANICS AS LAST AMERICAN LEAVES.' 'ANGRY PICKETS LASH TOP JOCKEY WILLIE.' And in a heavy Dutch accent, *Algemeen Dagblad* announced: '*KANS OP CRISES BLIJFT!*'

To keep up with the rest of Europe, the crime rate in Málaga has risen; port of call, furlong, of blind men, of graveyard statuary, ornate chess-sets. In La Sirena fish-bar by the harbour the well-heeled clientele are flashing 5,000 peseta notes, not bothering to count the change. The barmen move as elegantly as dancers. Bar Pombo is closed for good. The lottery-man is whistling the opening bars of Beethoven's famous Fifth, the so-called Symphony of Destiny. Blind men go tapping around the cathedral; inside the Orquesta Sinfónica de Málaga are offering *Ars antigua* (R. Diaz) and *Sinfonía sevillana* (J. Turina). Resident organist Christian Baude.

When the offices empty the port hums like a beehive. A vast Soviet tanker lies to in the bay. The wine-bars open. Deviants lurk in the groves of the Alcazaba. In certain tall hotel rooms overlooking stairwells you would suppose yourself back in a previous century. Port of curious chess-sets, stonemasons, shoeshine-men selling lottery tickets on the side, vendors and deviants, blind men, operatic traffic policemen in navy blue uniforms with white gloves and white pith helmets, sunglasses *de rigueur*, even in dark bars. Quiosco los Periquitos. Black swans with red bills paddle the dirty pond in the Alameda Gardens where a child dressed as a diminutive bride is being photographed by her adoring *papá*. It's time for lemon tea. Awkward soldiers with close-cropped heads are walking their girls. The sun coursing through the luxuriant overhang of tall palm trees lights up the inverts who watch from public benches. Not a crestfallen buttock in sight! *¡ASPIRINAS ASPROMANIS!* The cathedral bell at midday. *¡EXPLOSIVOS RIO TINTO!* Drawn by repetition of clever moves, White cannot escape the checks without letting the Black rook join the attack. And if his king tries to hide on 93, we may expect trouble. Platonou and Minic wiped off the board. *Adiós* Quinteros and Browne! The *mariposas* are in a perpetual froth of excitement in the clever mazes of the Alcazaba; lured by the stagy décor, the sudden appearance and disappearance of like-minded lads. *Todavía no me acostumbro estar frustrado.* So much, as Plato politely phrased it, for such matters.

While modern Spain sprawls along the Mediterranean, busily going to Hell, the ascending new road to Ronda is as extraordinary as the southern approaches to Barcelona. Cut off from the mess of the coastal 'development' and deep in the off-season, Ronda (850 *metros de altitud*; 32,049 *habitantes*) offers herself as a kind of Sparta. A bullfighter's town. From here came Pedro Romero and the great Ordoñez.

The coastal stretch from Málaga to Marbella is as ugly as the urban development from Salthill to Costello Cross on Connemara's Atlantic seaboard, allowing the Spaniards slightly better taste. Up here men with windscorched faces are talking intently to each other. They are addicts of circles and all shades of green, with the habit of contradicting you ingrained, a Moorish trait. In Ronda your thoughts fly upwards. Walk on the windy walls. To live here would be to marry a very strict but beautiful woman.

The surrounding countryside of undulating hills and far vistas rivals certain valleys in Yugoslavia near the Austrian border, or the Transvaal. Beyond the gasoline station (Zoco 500 *metros*) lies the veldt; land the colour of puma, Africa.

And do they love green! Oxidized bronze bells, washed and bleached army uniforms of Thai-like neatness, worn with panache under tasselled forage caps, introduce touches of green everywhere. Into the Bar Maestro – just wide enough for you to turn around – twitches a grievously afflicted beggar, calling '*¡BOOoojijjji!*' In an alleyway off a nameless street a bar is crammed with soldiers in green uniforms. 'PEÑA TAURINA ANTONIO ORDOÑEZ', the sign says, swinging in the wind. A torture-picture: the sad comedy of a reunion of friends.

In Piccola Capri, open at long last, the recorded voice of Bob Dylan sounds like an unhinged aunt, singing sadly over a sensational view of the gorge by night. Down there tumbles the Tagus.

I see a line of hanged victims carved in stone. In the pedestrian walks you see the finite gestures of bullfighters, jackets draped over shoulders in *torero* manner when the weather permits. The wind sets its teeth into the *toreros*-to-be, the Ronda girls rumpy as *rejoneadores*. This shoulders protrude like flying buttresses. Mauve slacks are worn by these addicts of *alegría* who spit *pipas* in the street; flashers of *mil* peseta notes, dislodgers of preconceptions, relishers of large mushrooms sautéd in garlic, child-lovers, they themselves somewhat childish. A chess competition takes place in what once must have been a Moorish palace. *Peña: J. M. Bellón. Torneo Social Ajedrez.* For three days the Levant blew a half gale.

Men with convex eyebrows frown thoughtfully into their coffee and Cognac. '*Poco diferencia,*' they say, always ready with the qualifiying clause, the caesura, the direct contradiction. I have two eyes, I say to the man in the late-night bar (we are discussing the 'invisible villages'). No, he says, you have four. It's true, I'm wearing *gafas*.

An old church, I say to the old man in the corner of the

librería where I buy carbon paper. No, he contradicts me, not old, only two hundred years – of Iglesia Nuestra Señora del Socorro.

In the Germanic Restaurant Jerez near the bullring a distinguished grey-haired man arrives with a lady in furs. The owner seems to know me, hovers about our table and stares pointedly as if at a long-lost son who refuses to acknowledge his own *padre*. The noble-looking Frenchman in the neck-brace, hair a sable silver, pulls up his expensive tweed trouser-leg to expose a calf of corpse-like whiteness to the lady in furs who bends forward, slowly removing her sunglasses – '*Ouch, chéri!*'

In the long bar overlooking the plaza a stout man in a Panama hat set at a bullbreeder's angle sits at the counter, plunged in thought. He is joined by men in expensive leather jackets, with the swarthy faces of impresarios. A posse of purposeful men with bursting bellies now arrive, roaring for *cerveza*.

A calm nun in a powder-blue modern habit is transacting some business at the Banco Central. The waiter with the scorched face above his red jacket is playing in an old Simenon thriller, as is the lovely girl who sold me carbon paper in the *librería*, as is the contrary old man sitting in the corner. A thin bell is tolling. The cold in hot countries is absolutely poignant.

The bullring is the largest and most dangerous in all Spain. The New Town is a mess, a sort of Arab shanty-town. A ring of towns with odd names face Portugal: Estepa, Eciza, Arcana. On the winding road to Marbella and the desecrated coast lie the 'invisible villages'; not to be missed on any account.

Soon the eastern coastline from Estepona near Gibraltar to Gerona near the French border will have gone the way of Marbella and Torremolinos, and it will be left for hardy souls to move to Pontevedre or La Coruña on the Spanish Atlantic coast. American bombing colonels out from the air-base at Morón de Frontera drink Cognac like beer.

Over Ronda hangs a most Moorish moon and I never wish to leave it.

It is a creepy place.

The intense light shed at noon in winter can produce an unhinged effect, like walking on water; a mescal dream on beer or gin – living as flying. Scandinavians now run bars (Bjarne) or manufacture ice-cream (Bjorn), being an adaptive race out of their own country. The Irish Bar is run, wouldn't you guess, by a quiet Englishman.

Two truculent sailors from Dundee are huggermuggering at The Anchor. In the neon-lit surreal night a passive crowd of mixed nationalities, a little lost, go perambulating; an army of street entrepreneurs attempt to gain and hold their attention, always flagging, afraid of being done, moving on. Grisly prints are everywhere on view.

Here is a town of shifty characters always on the move. Flat at first, just a throughway, it becomes suddenly a maze of levels with flights of stairs descending; regions of mugging and lush-rolling. Keep your wallet buttoned up. In the English Bar, run by a Plymouth couple, an oil-tanker crewman, who likes to play a bit of golf, says that being cooped up for months on end in the belly of a big tanker can make a man go all funny. Has he come to the right place? Would not a fortnight here be tantamount to spending fourteen days and nights trapped in a Ferris wheel whirling? But people seem to like noise today, need it; silence augmenteth rage. We live in peculiar restless times.

Whores and pimps abound by night. Discos thunder, strobe lights flash, recorded voices bellow. The young are packed together in dark underground cellars; pay as you order, the light is poor, the recorded sounds deafening. I am offered a small sullen girl by a large Bavarian pimp in sombrero; seemingly quite at home (Schwabing?) in these Andalusian badlands. The quick turnover. French is spoken by the questing pimps.

Architecturally the place is a true nightmare. Grouped along the shore and turned inwards upon themselves high-rise apartments of depressing sameness appear to advance

136

seaward – a breeding place for crime. It is a manner of building – one cannot call it a style – that suggests impermanency. Strange factor in a building, concreteness rotating towards illusion. Johannesburg or Salisbury in Zimbabwe: poverty does not exist, provided you rise above it. Pie in the sky. Corbusier fathered this inhumanly scaled grid patterning, these elevated box-quarters piled on *ad nauseam*, offering an unreal cycloramic future in the here and now. Odd that a Frog should make such an error; a building style designed for transients, commercial travellers, call-girls, night-owls. On twenty-first storey terraces behind the high-wire fences Modular Man plays tennis for ever and ever.

Unamuno's 'ether of pure speculative contemplation' has no place here; but look away, not far off are wooded mountains and a lake, where few people go. Of the old village, the Tower-by-the-Sea, little remains, the market being the only authentic part left. But why are *gambas* so expensive? The Mediterranean fished out already? They used to be given away free with draught beer in Málaga.

Latins, the multitudinous forms of machismo; the gushing fountains, the bullring.

Multitudinous? Come, come; say rather the stereotypes. Behind Andalusian machismo lurks the Moor. Although departed several centuries – the fall of Granada and the discovery of America occurred simultaneously – in the body, some of his nature and character remains; the residue of his language, the ruins, his shadow. The Alhambra presumes inner space. And the true notion of the dignity of man is that all are extraordinary, at least potentially. A deeply Spanish conviction, this, not I think found in the doleful Gaelic philosophy of *An scath a chéile a mhaireann na daoine* (people live in one another's shadows or are dependent upon one another). Midway between Málaga and Nerja lies the tax *refugio* of Torre del Mar with a powerful stench of open drains. Its foreshore looks as grim as the Mexican wasteland of Buñuel's *Los Olvidados*. It has become a German colony. Hoffman's zone of empty

137

high-rise apartments awaits more Germans from the cold hard cities of the North. A beach has been cleared and named; it will look fine in a colour brochure. A brothel has opened at Nerja.

From the mouths of mercenary men in the Bar Don Quixote the word *negocio* drops like mercury. Wads of *mil* peseta notes are flashed. Cured hams hang from the low ceiling. Dick and Tony have retired to Málaga. Two stout German *Fraus* with gross backsides packed tight into white flannel slacks pass by in the subdued company of a stout *Herr* with a nervous French poodle on a lead. A plump *Fräulein* in a pink bikini as brief as decency will permit walks along Burriana beach with a brownskinned local manikin who is not right in the head; his features are squeezed together into a veritable snout. They go linking. Two dogs are copulating in a cove, observed by amused German sunbathers.

Again the constants: English hopelessness, German pushfulness, both lost in a language they will never learn, a culture they do not wish to know.

'How's our Kitty?'

'Are you near the end?' an exhausted female voice asks to my right, on the Balcón de Europa.

'Time to go back for lunch,' an elderly male voice answers, *sotto voce*.

At La Luna on the outskirts of Nerja (population 6,000 ten years ago, 16,000 today) bronzed German couples play tennis on the municipal courts. In the bar a Yorkshire JP, late of Burma, says he believes in capital punishment. Bring back the birch. He is for hanging Provos.

On the plateau, which ten years ago was a scrubland for the passage of goats to the river below, now has arisen a monstrous development of high-rise apartments. When the sun goes down behind El Capistrano, 300 Belgians stand on 300 identical balconies, watching it sink, before retiring indoors to flush 300 identical toilets.

The signs are up: 'PROHIBIDO' . . . 'PRIVADO'; the guard-dogs alert, the sprinklers working – it might be a Capetown suburb. Jesús has sold his fish restaurant and gone horse-riding in the hills. Paco Fernandez, son of an honest banker, is erecting a Mussolini-style mansion on Calle Carabeo on top of the poor quarter; an ingenious way of effacing want. Lady Blanche is in *constant* correspondence with the grandson of Richard (*Gatherings in Spain*) Ford. She has no trouble at all in understanding the mystery of the Blessed Trinity.

The Parisian psychoanalyst who dabbles in oils has painted a black bull that would pass for a black astrakhan hearthrug, such as might adorn the living-room of Germans who decorate their heavy rich apartments from the advertising sections of *Bunte* and *Stern*. Businesswomen are selling insurance and steel tubing.

'Psychic death,' says the subtle Doctor Klaus from Berlin. Voodoo is back, the Evil Eye, witchcraft. He himself has a heart condition, being a gluttonous eater of meat, hardly reassuring in a doctor of medicine; would *you* be treated by a blind oculist?

'Most discoveries are economical,' says the homeopathic doctor, who claims to have cured his own multiple sclerosis and can cure yours, at a price; having refused no less than five chairs at Gröningen. He hopes to open a sanatorium in the hills, become its Hofrat Behrens. He believes that the Soviet Russians are infiltrating Europe and have already taken secret control of Scandinavia. 'I started clearing up my kidneys with parsley soup.'

'CUEVAS DE NERJA — FANTASÍA NATURAL', the sign says. But is it not the town itself, grown so monstrously, that is the unnatural fantasy? El Capistrano, the clotting on the hill overlooking La Luna and the river, is a village in Spain the way a Butlin's camp is a village anywhere. T-shirts bear the name, so that the inmates of Casa Cost Enuff can recognize a friendly neighbour. Half the face has been cut off a mountain to make a quarry, and the construction trucks run all day. The main lingo of the beaches on Costa del Sol would seem to be German: '*Fleisch*' chalked above '*porc*' and 'meat' on the menu boards. A sinister breed of

Germans have come down to the coast from Hamburg, Hanover, Essen. The vicious Bremen hippy is living with his seraglio near a waterfall on the way to Frigiliana. A morose German owns the *merendero* on Playa de Salon, serving German-style mugs of cream with coffee *dobles* for 62 pesetas to some early-risen English couples who speak in intense and compromising vagaries.

'How's Fritz and Kitty?'

'I know this for a fact because I've got friends in the Forestry Commission myself.'

For emphasis, the English lower their voices. Germans raise theirs. The favoured mode of address among Spaniards would seem to favour the half-shout, even when standing within touching distance.

On Burriana a group of idlers are much diverted by the antics of a *mono* on a lead, dressed in Turkish trousers and a red toque, diminutive, almost one of themselves but not quite. *Können Tiere Lügen?* Can animals lie? Of course not.

A gaudy macaw leers from a cage suspended over Calle de la Gloria. The asters have withered on the columbarium where Miguel Rojaz sleeps his last sleep in the *cementerio*, with a fine view of the Cuesto del Cielo, over which shadows of passing clouds fall obliquely: *testimonio recuerdo*.

Over the swimming pool in the garden of *número* 32 Calle Carabeo Old Glory flies above the Spanish tricolour on the masthead, in the house now owned by one of the Rothschild brothers. We lived there once.

Behind Burriana beach the exploitation goes on, new roads cut out of the ochre sandstone, building sites laid out. The drains cannot take all that's been put into them. Stink of fish on the sand below the *parador*, stink of diesel oil offshore. Windsurfing must be the last late-twentieth-century distraction that is soundless; figures flying and floating prophetically out of da Vinci's sketch-pads into the here and now. The Mediterranean has a nip in it in early May and few venture in. On a stalled pedalo off the Balcón de Europa within full view of all, a beast is forcing his attentions on a beauty in a *very* brief mauve bikini. Her scream hangs over the water. The tick-ridden stray dogs who have had a dip are now pissing against the rocks; soon to be observed complacently by the sunbathing German group, strenuously copulating in a cove. At mid-morning a band of male Germans are roaring drinking-songs at Pepe Gomez's *merendero*. Where Leslie Marshall ('a very common name in Scotland') confides his fear of the wily Russians. 'The Rooskies are past masters at dabbling in troubled waters.' He recalls a Singapore brothel with a cherry tree bursting through the roof and the madam presenting him with a toothbrush wrapped in cellophane on leaving. It was 1937 and he was young. Now he's a dead ringer for James Joyce. The Nerja bordello stands behind the church. A local rapist out of prison knows the ropes there; 2,000 pesetas a knock.

On the five beaches sun-bronzed Prussian widows of advanced years and flab go topless; sights for sore eyes, *nichts für ungut*. The pretty French and German girls also, sunbathing and swimming, suffering themselves to be kissed topless and generally move about as if in Eden and not in the Turdy Pleasure Grounds. In the prone position when oiled for sunbathing, the top of the bikini may be entirely removed and the bottom part pulled down as low as decency will allow; what Swift termed the dishonourable part may be fairly exposed. A young lecher wearing a peaked cap is on the prowl, armed with powerful binoculars.

On Carabeo beach the pretty long-haired tease who came skipping down the path with hair freshly washed is now perched elegant as a mermaid on a boulder and lighting up a Marlboro; presently to be metamorphosed into Mariposa the gay barman who mixes a strong Bloody Mary.

At Io's *merendero* the waiters run. Flies are dancing in the *servicios*. Petting and kissing occurs in the most public places, behaviour that in Franco's day would have resulted in jail sentences and even deportation.

Spaniards are given to hyperbolic excess; with them,

silence is a form of impoliteness. The constants remain: stink of drains, the morning parade to Burriana. The helplessness of the English and the rudeness of the Germans; French *elán*, finickety manners, they turn *café-au-lait*-coloured in the May sunshine, the non-Latins go lobster-red, tumescent. Large Labradors and Alsatians strain at stool in public places. A smart Spaniard drives past the Banco Atlántico with a credit card clenched between his teeth, both hands on the steering column, the ultimate in chic. (The English like to be seen entering bars with car keys on leather tags held between the teeth.) The fish-bar smells vaguely of fresh vomit.

It's the dead hour of the day in Andalucía, four in the afternoon; not much life stirs in the Bar el Kiko or the Bar Julian. The redheaded barman, who looks Irish but is a local man, helps himself to a quick shot of Terry in the swanky bar of the Hotel Balcón de Europa. A well-fixed native son is just wiping his Citroën in the forecourt of Apartamentos Playa de Torrecilla, which is owned by an Englishman. Rafael Fossy counts his night's poker takings laid out on his bed: half a million pesetas. The Aerolitos are giving out their dire space gruntings. An elderly boozer with hare's teeth and a squashed straw hat with a broken band is sipping red wine in the Bar el Santos. The engineer Manuel Herrera Bueno of Calle de las Angustias is without a job.

Alberto Joven the barman, who can speak four languages, addresses me as *¡Compañero!*; a great honour, coming from this human dynamo. I, the feeble *escritor*. He copies out the Octavio Paz poem that begins '*Controlador de serenos esclavizas . . .*' Reads it back to himself.

'This man is not happy,' he says. *Polvo* (dust, powder) in context has 'a metaphysical meaning'. If there is such a thing as the dignity of the working man, Alberto Joven personifies it.

Women seem to age better than men. Possibly they take better care of their bodies. The men don't give a damn, exposing hairy pot-bellies, the sagging paps of Tiresias. All

women are not Helen, I know that; but all women hold
Helen in their hearts. Strawberries are in. May lightning
has blasted a tree in Berkshire, I am told. But the Land of
Lotería is changing. Meaty hand-clapping drives intelligence
out of the head. An eagle-owl staggers out of the sea. The
búho real!

Which leads us back by a commodious vicus to the slaugh-
terhouse all white tiles inside, a cow, a goat, two bleating
kids, and a pig, along with some very innocently dressed
butchers, that is no costume, not even work-a-day don't
you know the informal touch, all grist to their mill, those
gruesome things, *herzlich, mit freundlichen Grüssen*, sharpest
knives in town, and the pig put up the best fight.

Dumb brutes they, all slosh and this and that, a view of
the fields, the last view, a cauldron for shaving off the skin
I suppose. Smiling faces gentle men, takes all types these
days to remember anything, just guts and great swirling
forms, start to see the abstract positive and negative, the
throat takes, the tongue swells, but not until you get your
right elbow halfway down the pig's throat groping for the
heartstrings will the thick beast let go its life. No music if
you please, I've got a timid system, inherent dizzyness and
garlic fillet with a stiff glass of beer or two, elbow at sides,
yes even now I can taste the sour refrain.

The man's all a-shake now how nice, a family bag
secured tightly above the ears, leather I think, a young
Scorpio friendly to the very end suggests I put something
on my head, well there it is. I think the leather to absolutely
muffle the screams, effective just as your arthritic itch of
ageing relatives, cleaned in a damp toilet twice a year.

One eye going out here, the other there, almost defiance
when you would fancy a look of trepidation, well that's
not the way of the beast, no sir, beginning to cough up the
innards. The least I could feel for the poor dead things
hanging by their hooves down by the river which is named
River of the Occasional Yelp in Spanish. Well of course
that's inaccurate, like most things, but the suggestion is

certainly not far from yelping dog. Found a dog eating away, some spare intestines I supposed. And the hung things, the carcases don't you know, bleeding away, bleeding away.

Our coach overtakes trucks loaded to capacity with orange *butano* containers, for cooking Spanish dinners, two racing cyclists in yellow and blue caps marked 'FIAT', going like hammers of hell, overtaking each other in quick bursts of speed, driving down hard on the pedals, speeding freaks from Jarry's *Supermale*. Heading for Valencia, that town of good white wine, swaying palms, wildly gesticulating heroic statuary. A spring is released and then something snaps; the freed spirit soars.

We pass orange groves protected by windbreaks of cyprus, pines about olive groves, peach interspersed with vines, the succulent South, a line of racing hills. Pine-covered hot hills, water-cannons firing in a green field by sugar-cane plantations, three tiers of young porkers in a well-ventilated scarlet trailer bowling merrily along towards some distant abattoir. I have set out from Málaga to travel to Barcelona, 200 kilometres away, and then 170 to the French border, passing through Paris at night, reaching London on the third day.

Pylons now, orange flames shooting up from gas refineries into the clear air, the tall striding shapes of praying mantis are building cranes, the signs and symbols of modern industrial Spain. A series of linked motorways, *salida* 35, toll-gates, tall cyprus trees in a cemetery passing, some haciendas, more palm trees buffeted by the wind, another flyover. B141, a sign seemed to convey, REUS, TARRAGONA, VALLS.

French cars heading for the border (do they arrive as fast as they depart?), Port Bou, Biarritz, racing by a fine aqueduct outside Tarragona. French drivers are dangerous half an hour before lunch and even more so before dinner. Dutch drivers are helpless in the Alps. But the approaches to Barcelona are as exciting as the approaches towards any modern city. B97.

One approaches it by long easy spirals, with Spanish prosperity becoming more evident by the minute, unlike the straight run into West Berlin across the grim DDR and its darkness before the blue neon Schultz signs. The hoardings began 82 kilometres out as the flyovers became more frequent, the toll-gates. Did a racing sign say 'BARAMAR'? Sitges sounds like an infirmity, not a place, and Vendrell is hardly an improvement. I see a pith helmet and a bottle of VAT 69 in the back seat of a German Lancia; blue-domed churches are left behind and the late-afternoon air becomes cooler. An intermittent stench rises off the chemical-dosed land. The sky is alive with feeding swallows. A sign cries 'LA CAIXE!'.

A fine church dome, as if dancing, is left behind with a whiff of perdition off the land.

PINORD . . . KENT . . . SKOL . . . BARCELONA 45 . . .

The city's lighting system begins. Off to the right are the new towns, Villanueva and a tormented anagram: Geltru. Beyond lie Badalona, Matard, Tossa de Mar, San Feliu de Guixols, Cadaqués, Patmos, the drums and spheres and flames of oil refineries, Olympia Nuclear SA, the piled-up drainpipes of an expanding city.

The courier gives his spiel patiently. We are booked into the Hotel Apolo in the Ramblas. Take all you need for the night. Dinner is on the company. The call is at 7 a.m. We depart 8.15 for France with two French drivers who will remain with us until London.

The coach goes accelerating into the city alongside a river. The first street-signs loom, 'LIV AUTOMATICA'; the tentacles of the city close around us, we have become part of a larger traffic movement. It's 5.30 rush-hour, September 15th. My feet have swollen. The ageing gay tour-guide, with his arm about a young puzzled boy, assigns rooms. 'We'll put Iggins wiff the Norwegian.'

I go drinking with Bjorn Engen (Angel Bear), who has buried two wives in Denmark, left the heavy tax and the

145

dead wives behind him to start manufacturing ice-cream in Torremolinos. The riot squad are out in the Ramblas, armed like combat troops. No more villainous-looking armed fellows had I seen since the sallow-faced American army troops went on parade in West Berlin. Last week a girl had been shot dead in a street demonstration. Watch your wallet in the Ramblas. Don't run.

Morning departure as per schedule. France lies ahead. The French drivers go with the expected panache, windows refreshingly open. The two dare-devil Spaniards liked to supervise refuelling with lighted cigarettes glowing under their mustachios. The rivers run with waters under splendid bridges. After the ordered fields of Perpignon the road-markings become long white Gallic lines with sporty stipple effects, Toulouse coming up with red and black ovals, curved roadsigns.

The cones of the red-and-white wind-indicators are straining away from the motorway. After Arles Spain begins to seem grubby. At Aix-en-Provence the roof-tiles change their contours: convex to the south, concave here in the north. A coloured dwarf with a long university scarf wound around his neck waits by the roadway alongside a travelling-bag twice the size of himself.

Motoring with Mr MacAuley

1984

Heathrow–Vancouver

Anything for a change, or a good laugh. Away from old austerities, the braying of loud-hailers and bull-horns as the winter of strikes and industrial unrest wears on, gives way to spring. Even the gravediggers downed tools.

A fig to all Tories! (a word which in the old Gaelic meant 'robbers'). Thumbs down to Jim Callaghan's mob. 'A shower of pigs,' the chatty London cabby threw over his shoulder. 'No self-respecting working man would vote for Mrs Thatcher.' Hadn't she withdrawn the free milk from schools, taken it from the kids?

To the Sunshine Coast, to the Sunshine Coast! At the behest of the Canadian Association for Irish Studies (CAIS) and the University of British Columbia (UBC), joint hosts of the 'educators and other interested parties', for the Twelfth Annual Conference at UBC in far-off Vancouver.

To this jamboree were invited Dr Conor Cruise O'Brien ('Statesman and Writer, Dublin') and a mixed bag of minor academics, historians and authors, among whom your humble.

Heathrow–Vancouver non-stop via Air Canada and our number already coming up on the board. Departure at 14.30 and arrive the same mid-afternoon in Vancouver, flying against time and the sun on the polar route.

No one meets me at the other end, in a clean and strangely deserted Vancouver International Airport. Taxi uptown; the hotel is booked up but the obliging desk man phones another within walking distance. Weak in the Mayo knee I haul my bag there. High-summer air, palms and balmy breeze, sails tacking across blue water. I book into the Sands Motor Hotel on English Bay. A Japanese receptionist takes my Irish passport, assigns a room. A long, low first-floor room with a narrow view of the anchorage. I change out of sticky clothes. Heavily chlorinated water opaque as pulque gushes from the taps; it's like showering under a cataract. In a fourth-floor room in a block of flats opposite, a young couple jitterbug in a time out of mind. Joggers with long suntanned legs trot by in the street below. Presently a sensational sunset framed between blocks of buildings; mooring-lights of shipping in the bay, and so, nursing my knee, supperless to bed.

The Vancouver morn reveals to me: street-cars leaving punctually for Main, two postal deliveries within the hour, a man sweeping up blossoms, tall beauties on their way to work, one holding a flower. I phone Philip Moir at the university, where a secretary addresses me as 'Professor Higgins'. Check out; taxi to campus, check in. Professor Roy Foster of Birkbeck College signs the register just ahead of me. We are assigned rooms in the Theological Faculty.

UBC is set, lush as botanic gardens, on over four hundred hectares of land by the Pacific, and takes in the Nitobe Memorial Japanese Gardens, the Rose Garden, a Museum of Anthropology, with a fine collection of that fugitive thing, Coastal Indian Art, and an Olympic standard swimming pool. It's vacation time; the handsome campus pleasantly free of students and their graffiti, the subversive aerosol squirt so common elsewhere.

The Belfast dramatist John Wilson Haire, late of the Royal Court, and Stewart Parker with *Spokesong* behind him, open the proceedings at International House, Ann Saddlemyer in the chair. An expert (Toronto) on the calligraphy of W. B. Yeats asks witty rhetorical questions from the floor. Parker is urbane; Haire tortured. Their subject: disunited Northern Ireland, a sore topic.

At the informal luncheon that followed, a bluff Canadian spoke at some length, presumably using a single utility all-purpose speech, of Red China's highly defective educational system, with sneers at Chairman Mao; a bravura piece of irrelevance that induced sniggers behind menu cards and some furtive note-passing, the first signs of hysteria. No drink was served. Buy your own at the bar. A young Brünnhilde came and sat by me. Drizzle and mist came down.

What lesson had Chairman Mao and his Red China with its teeming millions for the Emerald Isle and its few million inhabitants? No one seemed to know; while the bluff speaker droned on the man who could have put him right was absent. For the Irish contingent would be without the redoubtable services of Dr Conor Cruise O'Brien (an island unto himself), not one man but three as his Irish enemies averred maliciously; thought to be in France. He sent his apologies; as did the Irish minister, from Geneva.

Novelist and *raconteur* Ben Kiely and poetess Eavan Boland, daughter of former walrus-moustache Minister for External Affairs and perennial butt of *Dublin Opinion* cartoonists, did not show up, nor did Máire Mhac an tSaoi. A. Norman Jeffares, without whom no cultural conference can ever be quite complete, was also conspicuously absent.

A singular German linguist from Hamburg lamented the passing of the Manx language, as the rain came tumbling down. After all the speakers had had their say the Faculty Club did brisk business. $1.45 Canadian for English gin and tonic, $1.90 for Tuborg, served by tall bar-girls in black taffeta. Slacks and jeans came in baggier fashion than the skintights preferred in Berlin, Paris, London.

Back to the Agenda.

Tall men with assured public manners and long Presbyterian faces spoke of better times coming in the troubled province once called Ulster. They were putting up a case for a new history, a fresh deal. What with Belfast dramatists Parker and Haire, poet Paulin and linguist Barry, the Twelfth Conference at UBC was turning out to be a very Orange affair. The young-looking Professor Roy Foster had made little of his esteemed colleague's absence and read a long and witty paper on the vexed question of tenancy laws in the days of Parnell, the tolerant landlords of Co. Wicklow.

Some nervous Feminist ladies clustered on the podium like hens gathering on a roost, to deliver mercifully inaudible addresses into a spluttering microphone. The same, unfortunately, could not be said of a lady speaker who had come from New York to condemn *Ulysses* for its anti-feminist bile. She was to be seen and heard everywhere, coming volubly from the Ladies with a retinue of female admirers. *Moby Dick*, unfair to whales? The four Evangelists, unfair to mothers and whores?

Walked along the nudist beach and spoke to nudist father and small nudist daughter with minnows in a jamjar, took a dip in the Pacific, submitting to its odorous all-embracing female sexual pull. Tall spruce and pine grew close to the shore. In the tangle of thick undergrowth above rough youths could be heard cursing their Maker and smashing beer bottles on the rocks below, irritable as baboons.

Afternoon session at International House. An hour and more through which I would not gladly go again. Onto the podium slunk a smallish malcontent, said to be of Welsh extraction, an 'authority' on James Joyce. He read in a shifty manner not calculated to inspire confidence, consulting a large file, adrift in an argument purporting to be a new interpretation of that most transparent work, the *Portrait*, sending furtive glances into the body of the hall where an elderly white-haired man sat aghast, staring fixedly at the expert, who was now all a-tremble. None looks within himself where none can be. His halting remarks bore little relation to the novel one knew.

Some caustic questions from the floor, raillery disguised as flattery, were swallowed with a series of quick nods and convulsive grimaces, a gull choking on an outsize fish. Escape into the town for a meal in the Chinese Quarter.

In downtown Vancouver, Michel Tremblay's *Damné Manon, Sacrée Sandra* was playing at Spratt's Arts Theatre on Richard Street, an address the taxi driver had never heard of, come upon in a darkening street. Rain was coming in from Vancouver Sound and few pedestrians about. You can always see the sky in this hilly city.

Translated from Quebecois French, being the eleventh and last in a cycle that began with *Belles Sœurs,* the play was well into its run. The lovely Duchess of Malfi dressed in scarlet was waiting in the vestibule.

Décor: a triptych. A huge shadowy statue of the Blessed Virgin commands the back. On either side, large fridge doors that open to become the Gates of Hell. Clare Coulter as Manon, the female religious fanatic. Heath Lambert is the transvestite whore Sandra, togged out in toga-style white dressing-gown, slippers, fingernails and toenails painted viridian, the fungoid lips scream abuse, exuding a yellowish poison. The sagging jowls of Tiberias. With *Tartuffe* and *King Lear* behind him, *Travesties* ahead in Ottaway at the Vancouver Playhouse, Lambert gives an exceptionally baleful performance.

A religious play, then; supposing blasphemy can be accepted as a religious subject (Genet?). Sanctity has taken a wrong turning; kneeling can only induce lust. As the fungoid lips scream abuse the Doors of Hell fly open.

After the play the Duchess takes me on the town. We ascend by escalator to the lounge of the Four Seasons Hotel, served gin and tonic by waiters in scarlet tunics, among grottos and flowing fountains. Taxi to a party at Dr Jack Foster's, where the Duchess will be relentlessly pursued by the expert on Yeats's calligraphy.

Cascades, the Palouse

Eight a.m. departure from UBC in a thin rain, following party that ended at 5 a.m. Ann Saddlemyer and female friend waiting on the steps of the Theological Faculty, that quaint Gothic granite pile, for a taxi to take them to the Vancouver Island ferry.

I am to be driven by my new host, the genial MacAuley, to distant Cheney, moving out of deserted Vancouver on a Sunday morning, over Oak Street Bridge, on through the George Massey Tunnel, heading for Blaine on the US border, my first sight of America. Our route will take us through the Cascades, by North Cascades National Park and the Indian Reservations; by Grand Coullee Dam, to Cheney in eastern Washington State, at whose university I am scheduled to give readings. MacAuley pinches flowers from UBC campus for his wife. We breakfast outside the city.

First sight of true Americans on truly American soil: overfed armed customs men typing out passport details. MacAuley is excessively shifty. Passport pages are stamped; I must leave by such-and-such a date.

America: a long road, gum trees buffeted by wind, a deserted golf course. High thin cumulus. Curious contained smell in the foodstores; the smell of strangeness. Ah wilderness! Ameriky.

MacAuley wants to show me the Indian Reservations. Twice we will be stopped on the road by state troopers, the auto will be towed from the campus lot, MacAuley fined.

But now: Cascades, Concrete, Bellingham, Newhalem, beavers on the Skagit River. Winthorp, Twist, Otanagon, Omak, Nespelem, the Columbia River gorge. Hell's Angels have raced from California to the fake Western town where we stopped for lunch. The sheriff goes riding by in an open limousine as if stuffed; on his cropped bullet head a high stiff stetson. His overweight children follow him into the restaurant where we are offered processed food, a fish that is only a memory of fish, too-chilled lager, ersatz coffee served by a tease who hopes to get to England one day.

'Enjoy your meal!'

In the neighbourhood of Bridgewater another cowboy passes us in a pick-up truck. Tumbleweed fidgets across the dusty road, a huge valley opens out with cloud shadows moving over the hills, the wind blowing the topsoil away. A very old image: homesteaders' land and a dust-storm blowing topsoil away. Share-cropping, the most impoverished form of democracy.

'Where have all the people gone?'

'They haven't arrived yet,' MacAuley says.

By 1882, the year James Joyce was born in Dublin, the railroad had only reached Spokane; the early settlers were just arriving.

'And now?'

'Not much, as you can see.'

The wind rising over the Indian Reservation, poplars tossing in the Columbia River gorge, pylons on the march, cattle grazing across a plain, a hill flattened and ploughed for winter wheat, irrigated from the Columbia River. And the Redskins themselves, the first and last to understand the land, what of them? Gone long ago. A land settled by the white man for only a hundred years.

We drive on through the Palouse, the long road that leads to Wilbur, a catchment area a hundred miles long and one hundred and fifty wide, growing a fifth of the world's wheat.

A speeding Firebird with defective tail-light throws up dust ahead of us; two bored young couples are out for a Sunday ride to the Grand Coullee Dam. On this Sunday afternoon of luminous high clouds we are passing through the Palouse. We look down upon Electric City. The browsing brown cattle are 'worth their weight in gold', MacAuley tells me.

'French fur-traders came here in the early eighteenth century, trading with the Indians. They left their mark.'

On either side of the narrow road stretch the wide wheatlands. Winter wheat growing on exposed sites, wheat for Soviet Russia and China. Thin topsoil and scrubland over Pre-Cambrian granite.

'It's economial to put tons of fertilizer into the earth, spray crops with insecticides,' MacAuley says.

I look over the limitless wheatlands through which we

follow the road. A small barn owl flies across hunting mice. My erratic driver points out a SAC radar station on a hill to the right, pointed towards the USSR.

'In the event of threatening signs on the radar screens, counter-moves can be started within three minutes,' says MacAuley, with one hand on the driving column, gesticulating. 'Although when Nixon resumed his terror-bombing of Hanoi the Alert Pad was empty of B–52s. Make what you can of that.'

Wilbur, Creston, Davenport, Reardon, Deepcreek. To Spokane in the dusk; Cheney in the dark. Coming in we see the landing-lights of a huge B–52 playing touch-and-go on the tarmac and lifting off again. We keep moving. There are enough hydrogen bombs cached under a low hill to blow up the world twice over, my host informs me with American pride.

My lecturing/writing-workshop stint will last two days. Then off again, away again: Spokane, Seattle–Heathrow; to Kastrup Airport, Copenhagen.

His two young sons, excited by the arrival of a guest from over-sea, have stayed up. His present wife, the third, comes from the DDR; a nice pleasant solid lady greets me at the door.

In the John F. Kennedy Auditorium, moderator and writer-in-residence MacAuley intones:

'An international occasion . . .'

and I stand before a dozen enthusiasts for the written and published word, pens and pads at the ready, having come a long way for this.

I recall: the morning hummingbird in a chestnut tree, a glass of Scotch in the grass, the deckchair wilting in the heat of MacAuley's garden. Kildare Dobbs's witty speech at the UBC farewell banquet, his refusal to be distracted or put out of countenance by the rowdy Italian wedding party upstairs. The beautiful Icelandic girl who sang so sweetly to a harp accompaniment, the Gaelic-speaking excise officer who played 'Banish Misfortune' on the bodhran. Big Shirl the part-time bar-girl staring at me in the gloom of

the bar where I went with the reformed alcoholic. A
potential killer was drinking beer from the bottle; bandaged
American faces. The B-52s, the sound of their heavy passage
in the night. A bleeding hamburger which the young son
refused to eat. Black spots, said to be bald-headed eagles,
wheeling over the forest at Squamish on the estuary, Tom
Paulin a long way from Belfast, and chilled white wine in the
riverside restaurant full of trappers. Hot girls squeezed into
shrinkfit denim seated sexually on the mighty heated thighs
of scorch-faced muscle-bound fellows with blond cropped
hair, in a wooden bar that smacked of the coarse frontier.
The arms of the hot girls locked about the beefy necks of the
valiant escorts, all drinking beer, watching padded lunatics
on skates attempting to put their opponents through the
crash-barriers; violent sports on colour televisions never
turned off.

The hummingbird, the Scotch in the grass, Big Shirl. 'I
only eat hamburgers when I'm not hungry,' the young son
said.

Knowing it was over, and glad it was over. The last
adieus with MacAuley at Spokane Airport, following a
double gin strong enough to fell an ox; walking along a
narrow red carpet in the departure lounge.

'Catching kamploops,' quoth Harry Missildine of the
Spokanesman, 'is largely a matter of knowing where and
how.' On Monday, at the Spokane Country Club, I had
missed a rare opportunity of seeing Golden Bear, Jack
Nicklaus, play in an exhibition fourball. A crowd of four
thousand ('with few or no gate-crashers') had seen him
shoot a six-under-par 66, in the company of the no less
legendary Arnold Palmer (71), there with the remnants of
his army, Tom Watson (68) and local boy Rod Funseth
(71).

At a press conference before the game, Nicklaus had
been voted Athlete of the Decade. He 'rifled' off shots,
stroked the ball 'awfully close' to the pin with irons of his
own design, retaining the gallery's 'adoration' wherever he
went. In the *Spokanesman* photo the gallery looked overfed,

high-coloured cardiac cases. The colour had run, producing a squint effect, Nicklaus looking truly golden in Scots plaid trousers, a multimillionaire.

May 9th. 4.15 p.m., departure from Spokane Airport by Northwest Orient on DC-10 for Seattle. The carpet like a red throat. The fizz of gin. Changed 250 American dollars into 1,000 Danish kroner.

My flying companion, biochemist Loess Steele, consults charts, clocks without hands, mere points of time. The wings of the DC-10 tilt, the cabin is flooded with strange light, we pass over the spines of great mountains. A rich land unrolls below.

'Oh how lovely!' murmurs the biochemist.

An unctuous masculine voice speaks a pre-recorded message:

'Beverage service will be available throughout this flight.'

I order gin and tonic with a slice of lemon, not too much ice, introducing myself when drinks are served. Loess Steele is in transit from Philadelphia to Seattle. She has grown sons, takes vacations in the Caribbean. Across the aisle stubby female fingers write with an unpractised hand: *The benefit of home savings . . .* The studious young brunette studies business techniques, writes on a yellow scratch-pad, pressing the nib down hard . . . *is also yours with an AOD card.*

Seattle–Heathrow

It was summer in Seattle. Those passengers in transit seemed to know where to go, moving via unmanned lifts ('elevators') onto the various levels, where I am lost again, being a bad traveller. Even trams make me seasick. The faces at international airports tend to frighten. Too much world, too many Travel-*wütige* persons moving about. I am no poet of *Zusammengehörigkeit. Nein.*

In the unmanned elevator a pretty brownskinned young bride in a summer dress of wide-mesh white wool holds hands with her new husband, for they have the unmistakable look of newly-weds; perhaps married that very morning in Seattle, where it's always summer.

I find the Pan Am desk and am booked into Clipper Class on a B-747 to Heathrow. A fellow in exotic gear comes aboard with his duty-free trophies – alcohol, clothes, a span of antlers – bringing his loot in bursting plastic bags. How typical of the times, the measured level gaze of these pop types, aping their screen idols, McQueen, Bronson, Clint Eastwood. They have the mouths of consumers, rapacious young carnivores, a steely look. This exotic moves forward jokingly into First Class as though it were his God-given right.

My section is a third full; a seat by the window, legroom. Two English soccer fans settle down to a game of soccer on a board. An overweight young fellow breaks open a tin of fifty Stuyvesant, *mit* Miracle Filter, *alive* with pleasure. By Heathrow he will have smoked up half.

'Wotta thrashen!'

'Didden 'e then? Not 'arf!'

The B-747 is flying in a north-westerly direction at an altitude of 33,000 feet, at a cruising speed of 506 miles an hour. Clipper Ship *Rambler* totes a maximum baggage load of 680,000 pounds, given a lift-off boost of 30,000 pounds by Pratt and Whitney engine, I read on our flight chart. The American air hostesses smile toothily. I'm Joy, Fly Me. They seem to listen attentively to queries from passengers, but in fact neither hear nor see, moving in a trance along the carpeted aisles.

They are flying nurses, and the insulated tubular cabin a sort of free-floating hospital. Passengers who sit and sip drinks in soft reclining seats, or doze with closed eyes, wrapped in travelling-rugs, as if stunned, in catatonic bliss, are the patients or invalids in hygienic flying hospital beds, carried forward into space in a state of weightlessness, their needs gratified at the pressing of a button, summoning the smiling night nurse.

A curious light falls obliquely on lolling or dozing passengers. Presently all are geared up by the promised arrival of a meal.

'Did you wish something cold with your meal?' Beverage service. The coloured air hostess can be frosty. For dinner: steak, lasagne or chicken. A half bottle of Beaune with lasagne.

Flying again over the frozen wastes of northern Canada, now in the toils of a general election. Trendy Trudeau out here, Thatcher in over there. Far below, under the clouds, a frozen lake, then a series of frozen lakes, tundra merging into snowscape.

We pass over Lake Athabaska. Then winding Peace River and the Great Slave Lake. The light is going now on the wastes of that 'unthinkable first day' recalled by Mr Beckett. I speak to an American engineer who is helping to build a new military city in Saudi Arabia, that will take 75,000 personnel and cost nine million pounds, not dollars. Down below there, I ask, staring down into the darkness, is the place empty? No, he says. Two million people live and work there, trappers, oil-prospectors and the like, scattered about. By night you can see their fires. I look down. Minute spots of light.

We have been fired over the coast range, over the spine of the Rockies, over Nelson, Calgary, Grand-Prairie, Fort Providence, Yellowknife and Edmonton. We will pass over Greenland, a Danish possession, between Upernuik and Thule, where Dr Rasmussen suffered; over the Atlantic's shoals of hake, skate and herring. Will fly between Belfast and Stranraer, pass over the Pennines and the Cotswolds, then the Chilterns.

Daylight continuing but blinds drawn by the night nurses. Most of the passengers asleep. I walk the aisles between the sleepers wrapped in red travelling-rugs, study the flight chart, look down into darkness. It's the early hours of May 10th and somehow I have missed a day, will arrive in Heathrow a day late, arrive at Kastrup a day late. Am reading Margaret Atwood's feminist novel *Surfacing*. How these feminist females do carry on, always with bees in bonnet, chips on shoulder. She writes:

'I realized it wasn't the men I hated, it was the Americans, the human beings, men and women both. They'd had their chance but they had turned against the gods.'

Then it was morning again and I looked down upon a scene of ghostly splendour 33,000 feet below. In the clear frigid polar air a rocky snowbound hinterland revealed itself, in whose vasty depressions great frozen lakes lay frozen still forever, filled with a milky consistency about the ridged approaches to impassable mountains. Perhaps at ground level no human eye had ever looked on this, not even intrepid Knud Rasmussen? An endless snowscape extending as far as the eye can see, indented here and there with weals and wind-cuts, mammoth boot-tracks, striations like wind-scratches across permanently frozen lakes, locked between snow-mountains – Nature's sanctuaries.

The sun shone at a terrific Arctic angle on snow stockades the colour of silver foil; but none look down save children and myself. Wrapped in a red Pan Am blanket, the civil engineer is sleeping. The two English *futballists* have been invited forward to the Pop Star's birthday celebrations and are living it up in First Class. The Chainsmoker has capsized, his mouth half open, wheezing. The flight chart shows our route. We are passing over indented mountains. A vasty gorge. A lilac mist drifts by on the port side. An innocent blue sky, the slate-blue balloons of one's lost childhood, opens out; an early morning sky. The coloured air hostess murmurs 'Hot coffee' in my ear. Nothing better, with a tot of Cognac.

Presently in the breaks of cloud below, the Atlantic appears, like another sky. The Boeing 747 flies calmly on through this inverted sky.

The Opposite Land

1984

Arrival

It's overcast over England. We descend through murky cloudbanks; a drab land reveals itself below. The B–747 rolls in to the loading-bay.

In the arrival hall at Heathrow incoming passengers move in a daze, smaller than Americans, less colourful in dress, less self-assured in manner, paler than Canadians. Queues form up at the buffet. Service is slow, but presently the first pale, slightly moist ham sandwich is carried triumphantly past on a plastic platter smeared with mustard; also strange sausage-shaped objects like blown up condoms – 'bangers' are a national delicacy.

Drinking civet-piss in a soaking sweat, I try for a Copenhagen number but there is no reply. Passive as zombies, standing or seated, staring out of the long windows, pacing about, restless, those in transit put in time. At the bar – a sort of siding near the ever-ticking Arrivals and Departures board – a distinguished gentleman of colour orders a beer.

'Light or dark, sir? . . . er, ale or lager?' the poker-faced barman easily amends the gaffe.

Hortative headlines scream from the front page of an abandoned *Sun*. 'LIFE FOR MONSTER OF AA!' 'STARK TERROR OF RAPIST VICTIM'. The AA patrolman who had raped a stranded girl motorist stood 'ashen-faced' before a judge's wrath. Guilty of conduct that would have disgraced a 'primordial savage'.

I'm back in the horn-mad land of villainy. In this disunited kingdom ruled by two stern matriarchs, one autocratic, a distant queen, persiflage rules, disquiet

165

spreads, bigotry is abroad. 'Winnie' and 'Monty' having passed away, only 'Maggie' remains, all true monsters. 'Nessie' has been sighted again, surfacing in Scotland. Rooks are building high in the Somerset trees.

Thuggery and pro soccer engage all interests as exchange-fees move into the million sterling. Anything is possible on the downward path. Labour disputes alternate with mayhem and murder. Soccer hooligans are uneasily contained behind moats and barbed-wire stockades as in a POW compound; written about daily in the overly familiar parlance of the gutter press. But what is one to do? In the Midlands the cities are dying from within. Even the BBC radio serials are neurotic. 'She didn't like dreaming about a dead person.'

'Chat shows' are popular, a cheap form of commercial radio. The *Robbie Vincent Chat Show* on LBC is well calculated to set the fastidious listener's teeth on edge. Melanie of Maidenhead had the coil inserted last October and is still bleeding, what should she do? Oldish ladies flirt, the accents are various, posh to semi-literate, records of social disharmony and frustration. Robbie dispenses words of wisdom and advice.

Back in the departure hall a Mr Ledwich travelling to Munich cannot be found. And here again are all the travelling lovers and lost ones. They file by, dramatically silent or chattering like monkeys. The true new vulgarity of Britain, formerly 'Great', can best be studied at these airport entrances and exits. They go by:

the Hip Swayer,
the Exotic Tease,
the Busty Big Blonde,
the Lourer,
the Buoyant Bitch,
the Boy-Girl,
the Grey-haired Lecher,
Pouty Lips,
the Po-faced One,
the Misanthrope,

Hot Fudge,
the Pusher,
the Mule,
Mr Mountebank,
the Soul in Revolt,
the Hot-house Plant,
the Misfit,
Madame Majeska,
the Dark Note,
the Unhappy Vixen,
the Frightened Man,
the Jogger,
the New Suffragette,
Jump Suit,
Blow Job,
Gadfly,
the Sneaky Old Beldame,
the Gruesome Party,
the Fellow-Who-Couldn't-Get-It-Up,
the Spanking Colonel,
Judy Chalmers (endlessly *en route*),
the Mad Monk,
his wife,
the Rich Digger,
the Right Bitch,
the Pain in the Arse,
the Gorgeous Gael,
the Shrouded One,
the Missing Link (could it be Ledwich?),
the Sedulous Ape,
the Sullen Baggage,
the Right Prick,
the Priest in Plain Clothes,
the Old Crud,
the Hard Case,
the Booted Cuban (with Good-time Girl in tow),
the Rough Rasta,
the Grim Counterrevolutionary,

167

Mickey the Dunce,
the Sheep in Wolf's Clothing,
the Sheik of Araby,
the Girl from Ipanema,
the Merchant Banker,
the Anti-Christ,
the Après-Ski Exquisite,
the Sodomite,
the Israeli,
the Two-timer,
Embraceable You,
'Whispering' Golden,
'Silent' Busby,
William Faulkner's Double,
Joe Soap,
the Hard Man,
'Even' Stevens,
the Cad With the Pipe,
and the dead too, pacing gravely along, deep in private
conversation, or silent, wrapped in thought:
Podge Magee and Terry Butler,
Gerda Frömel-Schurmann,
Alex Trocchi,
and last but not least, pushing through the gates:
the AA Patrolman, and
the Girl Motorist,
and then a lone female dressed in black, high fashion not
mourning, booted, mysterious even unto herself – possibly
Bianca Jagger travelling incognito.

'COPENHAGEN' now appears on the departures board, the
flying digits fluttering by, faster than eye-blink, constantly
re-forming. My destination, after

MUNICH	14.40	BEA
BERLIN	15.10	BEA
NAPLES	15.20	BEA
MADRID	15.25	BEA
AMSTERDAM	16.00	BEA
COPENHAGEN	16.15	BA

168

In the duty-free shop a rotund little Japanese lady holds up a bottle of Harvey's sherry to the girl at the cash-register. 'Shilly?'

The girl shrugs her shoulders.

'Shilly-*shally*?'

The girl looks away. Mr Ledwich cannot be found. The atmosphere is already densely Danish. The daughters masticate gum like ruminants. And now, the long-awaited:

COPENHAGEN 16:15 BA NOW BOARDING

I am boarding among solid Danes. No fraternizing; all are glad to be returning home. For me a five-hour wait is ending, the fruitless phoning of your new number, the Heathrow pay-phone connection ringing in an empty flat. Where could you be? I'll go anyway. All aboard for Copenhagen! We are flying out on a lovely sunny May day. To Kastrup Airport. Is it near the city? We file aboard in an orderly Danish way, the two silent daughters still chewing gum.

At Kastrup Airport a quiet crowd of Danes wait behind the grille. I have never been here before. You are not waiting for me. At security an Oriental girl, possibly Chinese, goes through my bag, not looking at me, her hands unzip, probe, feel – *next*!

I share a taxi into town with two pederasts bound for Jutland. One is English. Jutland is the place, he tells me, it's so peaceful there. In the slanting evening light now a quiet port appears: København.

Young women in headscarves ride old-fashioned cranky black bikes along cobbled streets. The taxi drops the other two at Central Station and I go on to your flat at Øster Søgade. And there is the lake, the watery blue quadrilateral, with three swans flying in. You are not at home. No message. The mad landlady Mrs Andersen is most uncooperative; of your movements or whereabouts she knows nothing. I ask the taxi-man for a reasonable hotel.

At the Østerport Hotel opposite the East Station a Japanese male receptionist takes my passport, issues me a key, points. I traverse a number of narrow hotel corridors, all deserted, until I find a narrow room facing the railway tracks. If you do not show up, I vow, I'll leave for London by air tomorrow, even if we have not met in four years.

I walk out under a drifting sky, passing through the King's Gardens where Christian IV, 'the people's king', fell under the spell of a hard and beautiful woman, who let him down in his old age, went riding around with a guardsman instead, leaving the king to die alone with dropsy in his legs.

The transvestite carpenter works alone in the old street of whores. In the students' bars the style is to collapse footless across loaded tables and be set upright again, no apologies offered or required. The pimp for male prostitutes – a retired sea-captain – is guffawing away in the flower-shop. The Marxist translator of Marquez brawls in the bars, drinks Mateus Rosé at home with his new bride. In Copenhagen the telephone rings in muted tones, subdued as the taxi intercom, as the voices of the people. This quiet city suits me. The musical sing-song voices are telling me that already it has begun. I am here, so it must have begun. But where are you?

In Dyrehaven the moles burrow deeper. Baroness Blixen is buried under her favourite tree at Rungstedlund. Perhaps in spirit she is in the company of Denys Finch Hatton in the Ngong Hills with the lions, all lying down. This is the monstrosity in love, lady; that the will is infinite, and the execution confined; that the desire is boundless and the act a slave to limit.

Didn't you know? And where are you? How was I to know that you had gone to Elsinore Castle?

City of phantoms. Tired faces in May. Sailors on shore-leave. Groups of German students leaving in a launch for a trip around the harbour; a view of copper domes, ornamental snakes. They speak German, naturally; I may follow

170

them a little. In the streets Danish is spoken; this I cannot follow at all.

And where are you, my dearest? If I may call you that.

No lewd burlesque tonight at the Tivoli Gardens, where McEwan's Export play 'Hands Across the Sea'. Staid middle-aged citizens parade in green *Lodens* in the parks, the people pale-faced after the long northern winter. In general appearance they are a racial mixture of German and Dutch, but sober. Sober observers; they look you in the eye. Their eyes follow you.

A bronze statue of a tortured peasant sits with head bowed, arms bound behind his back with bronze leather thongs, being pulled part by his own weight, on the primitive torture-machine called *træhest*, a cruel Danish version of the old Saxon stocks.

Time passes. You arrive by night from Elsinore Castle. I leave the Østerport Hotel. In a small bar near a bridge, down steps, you order cold herring in aspic with Schnapps and Tuborg. A candle burns on the bar-counter. The woman who serves us is regal. You sit opposite me. Around us the port. The candle glows. Time passes. The ghost of Kirsten Munk drifts through the King's Gardens. Now that the people have left and the gates are locked for the night, all is quiet there. The night outside is quiet in a thoroughly Danish way; we have found this bar, this peace. After ten o'clock few pedestrians are about. The moon rises over the harbour. We return to your flat.

Then it's day again. We take a train from Østerport Station to Humlebæk, to visit Knud Jensen at Luisiana Museum. I open a window, the passengers stare critically at me. Danes do not like fresh air when travelling. We arrive at Humlebæk Station. It's not as I had imagined it. But what ever is? I am with you.

Jensen is away. You say you are hungry. Over the road is Humlebæk Inn, set among trees. We order fresh sole with chilled white wine, served by a dumpy little woman and set before us on green baize. Danish mourners pass our table, wish us good appetite. We take coffee and

Cognac outside under a tree. Over there, you say (point-
ing), lies the Swedish coast. I saw something white: a
nuclear station.

I taste Cognac. Do Danes and Swedes get along together?
No, you say, Swedes consider themselves superior. You can
speak Swedish fluently. Your Italian and English are adequate; now you are learning Greek. What more can you
learn? I order more coffee and Cognac. A man serves us
there under the trees.

In Humlebæk Kirke the jackdaws caw in a tod of ivy. On
the road, climbing the hill, a father passes on a pushbike
with his small son on the crossbar. The little boy licks ice-
cream and watches us as they pass, seeing a strange man
with a goatee and a tall lovely brunette pacing about in a
narrow cemetery of low box hedges, at Humlebæk Kirke.

From Humlebæk Havn we walked to the bus-stop, took
a number to Central Station. We bought Rioja wine and
returned to your flat. The days went by too fast, too fast.
The well-tortured peasant on the Wooden Horse has
expired at last. What could his offence have been, to merit
such a cruel death? Traffic moves either way over the
bridge at Øster Søgade. We were happy. Then came the
last morning. Four days.

How many facts does a life story require? What is fact
and what life story? It is not enough to live; no, you have
to know as well. Go on.

Then the last day came. We drank Elephant beer with
schnapps in Porno Street in the company of Jutlanders,
about whom you warned me. Beware their drunken rages,
their wild moves, their skinning-knives! Do not fall foul of
a Jutlander. But I saw only two peaceable men seated at a
small table with bottles of beer set out. A candle sent up a
thin spiral of smoke into the thin sunlight that came
slanting in. Behind the counter an old-fashioned radio
played muted Danish film music from the 1930s.

A third Jutlander now joined the other two; all three of
them were murmuring greetings, all wore woollen caps

172

and had hot, weathered faces. It was my last day. The last day.

Departure

In Central Station I prepared to go. We embraced. I won't look back, you said. Porters in brown uniforms, with fuzzy hair erupting from under caps too small for them, walked by the moving train in a possessive way peculiar to railway employees the world over. The boat-train was leaving punctually for Esbjerg Havn. You walked quickly out of the station, not looking back. Now you are passing over by the Østerport Hotel, from which I had booked out four days previously, on the same day as I had booked in, as the train began to pull out of the station, the fuzzy-haired porters walking alongside it, deep in conversation.

The fare seemed on the steep side. I found I was travelling First Class on a Second Class ticket in the company of a sour Scot called Dick Gaughan, late of Glasgow. The ticket inspector came; Gaughan paid the difference on two Second Class tickets. I would reimburse him when we stepped on board the boat for Harwich. The rest of the train was crowded.

Soon we reached the coast. At Esbjerg Havn the SS *Winston Churchill* was docked. We went aboard together. I found the exchange bureau.

We stood at the crowded bar. The dour Scot had been over for three nights at the Tivoli, three 'gigs' at £100 a time. They had cut a disc for their group: McEwan's Export. He was sick of Glasgow and planned to settle near Sligo. We drank Remy Martin and his mood improved. A shy, somewhat sour, good-hearted gingery Scot. We got on alright.

Hard rock thundered from two thunder-boxes controlled

by Tony Burton ('International Disc Jockey'). The metallic howling never let up, a male voice roaring out incomprehensible inanities, delivered at maximum pitch, the utmost volume, nothing human allowed to interfere. The Danish teenyboppers were galvanized, as though touched by electrodes. We ordered more Remy Martin. Don't forget your shovel if you intend to go to work.

For'ard, away from the howling disco, we came upon another more sheltered lounge, where middle-aged passengers were waltzing sedately. Here they could tango to their hearts' content. A male half-caste vocalist took the hand-held microphone and into the phallic head imitated a hysterical girlish high-pitched squealing. Gaughan and I began ordering doubles. Leaning on the bar counter my Celtic friend was moderately amused.

The SS *Winston Churchill* was hugging the unseen European shore. England seemed far away. Denmark receding. Clutching inebriated partners the dancers waltzed by, the half-caste continued squealing. Somewhere aft below the teenyboppers would rock and roll into the wee hours. I spoke to a fellow who had once spoken to Rex Harrison, when *he* was courting Lilli Palmer, my old heart-throb, then appearing in *Blithe Spirit* at the Golders Green Hippodrome. It was rumoured that Rex would return to play Professor Higgins in the West End at an estimated fee of one million pounds. And I would reach Harwich a day late, having lost a day re-crossing the North Pole, flying from Vancouver via Seattle on Northwest Orient, leaving behind sun and Pacific wind, the nudist beach, the big trees coming down to the shore, Japanese cherry in bloom, the opulence of Vancouver, the Chinese Quarter. I bade the dour Scot goodnight and retired.

At six next morning I was the only passenger stirring. The teenyboppers were flaked out all about me. An empty lager can was rolling about in the scuppers.

Just before midday the pilot boat *Valour* of London hove alongside. A vague ill-defined coastline appeared out of the murk on the aft side. Lowering vapours shroud the dim horizon. Could this be England?

Four jet fighters in tight formation tore the air to shreds above the SS *Winston Churchill*. The coastline began to drift by. Sealink passenger-liners followed each other towards open sea. Seaweed brushed past. A bell was tolling on a tilted buoy, a very old sound emitted now and then on the dirty swells. On the nearing coast a tall derrick rose up, then another. Dick Gaughan did not show up.

I recall: a bell ringing at a level-crossing, a stout Bornholm woman calling for Matthew, a herd of fallow deer, a man in forest-green crossing a path, the bellowing of the stag, shadows on the grass.

At Harwich I was first off. The boat-train was waiting. Two elderly porters with the complexions of jailbirds serving a long sentence, their uniformed shoulders with a fine dust of dandruff, began punching tickets in a listless English way. Hard-faced youths with convicts' close haircuts were leaning against the train, swigging tinned beer, on the lookout for 'birds'. Presently the boat-train pulled out of Harwich Station. Two Danish girls sitting opposite me drew three-tier Danish sandwiches from their holdalls. They offered to the mild air a pair of flawless complexions.

Their first view of England: a wayside cemetery with thin Anglican steeple above a granite church, rising into a grey thoroughly English sky. And, sliding by, schoolkids at horse-play on a station platform. A bully striking a weakling caught in the act of flinching away, his schoolbag falling. Bullies and frightened weakling, faces of another strange people, another race, petrified as on a screen.

I passed through a London of slanted sunshine and spring shadows moved now by balmy breezes, a new growth, come full circle. *Dine kys glemmer jeg ikke.*

Gas in the Decompression Chamber

1982

Few in their right minds could doubt that reality is two-thirds illusion in Iar-Connacht, the The-Bays-of-the-Ocean called Connemara. The Maamturks loom and recede, appear only to vanish, an optical illusion. The nights are still as the grave. Terrain so marine in nature, so embattled in history (defeat for the Irish), is entitled to its grave silence. But foxes are returning over the causeways built in Penal days, into Bealadangan, Annaghvaughan, Gorumna, Lettermore. The ghost of Sir Roger Casement coughs at night in the Hotel of the Isles, as the Atlantic wind rushes through the palm tree outside, and a miserable coal fire dies in the grate.

He dreamed of a free Ireland, a nation once again; confided to his diary: 'A world nation after centuries of slavery. A people lost in the Middle Ages refound, and returned to Europe.' But Ireland would never be part of Europe. An earlier historian noted: 'Thus separated from the rest of the known world, and in some sort to be distinguished as another world.' One female slave for three milch cows or six heifers. Between bouts of harsh coughing, Casement wrote: 'Individually the Englishman might be a gentleman, but has no conscience when it comes to collective dealing. Collectively the English are a most dangerous compound, and form a national type that has no parallel in humanity.' Waiting for him at their hands: the hangman's noose, Pentonville lime, posthumous disgrace. He liked dressing up, adopting disguises, travelling on false passports. He whitened his face with flour, buttermilk, travelled in a German U-boat with a cargo of sanitary pipes, was over-fond of his body-servant Adler Christensen, a man 'of atrocious moral character' wanted by the New York police.

Yesterday I watched a jackdaw being buffetted on a bough of the sycamore in Johnny O'Toole's well-set windbreak, cawing in annoyance or delight, who can say? Today, a loud assembly of crows there.

The low black devil-dog up the road, who had barked and run away, today crept onto the wall and suffered itself to be patted on the head – an even odder-looking beast when seen close up. A little girl emerged from the model Connemara house. Was it her little dog? Indeed it was. Its name? Elvis.

The O'Tooles were weeding in the windbreak. 'What's this ugly-looking thing growing over here?' Lucy asked her husband, the publican, raconteur, chain-smoker, historian, horticulturist and Fine Gael man. 'Nothing that grows is ugly.'

True enough. But little enough grows in Connacht (at least three-fourths of which is less than one hundred feet above the level of the sea), barring ancestral grievances. Lucy's father was a publican too, O'Connor of Salthill, doubtless related to the old ruling sept of O'Conor, former masters of Connacht.

'Whiskey' the Connemara pony stands all night sleeping in the frozen paddock, tail to the wind. In a remote bar in boulderstrewn Drim I was searched by three youths who said I was an armed UDA man, and they were Provos. Or Cowboys. The door was thrown open, I saw the darkness without. They pointed. In this out-of-the-way region, Ireland's old grudges take on some reality. But who is friend and who is enemy? Where in Iar-Connacht, the Celtic Katyn, does the old resentment end? 'Shoot the fucker!' a tall fellow stinking of draught Guinness bawls into my ear-lug. 'Down with the fucker!' The small devious smiling barman who had spoken with some feeling of King Herod's maggoty corpse, says 'Shussh!' but doesn't mean a word of it, taken with this display of patriotic ire.

'Shoot him! Shoot him!' howls the patriot, pint in hand, safe in this region of Provo sympathizers. The humid smoke-filled bar is in uproar. Cromwell and his dragoons ride down the unfortunate Pierce Ferriter, dispatch him with a sword-thrust through the third rib. Falling in slow motion Gibson of Ulster is tackled by a group of English defenders. Ireland are losing again, having defeated Scotland, and now face the old foe, who seem better trained, cooler headed, calculating, building their attacks. 'Get in the boot!' The narrow old bar by Lynch's Castle is steamy as a Turkish bath. Ward of Limerick is too late to take the pass, and down goes Gibson.

Then, breaking free from the ruck, the giant Kerry footballer Moss Keane takes possession and sets off alone for the enemy line, felling Sassanach to left and right; an awesome sight, and the bar goes wild. The dense air is friendly yet hostile, a *distilled* hostility. I drink hot toddies with cloves, half pints of Guinness. The rugby players seem to be struggling underwater, the scrums agitating the seabed.

Extraordinary clarity of the firmament above the little pier; in our Galaxie those remote small starres do reel in the Skie. In the morning the two hunting seals will come with the incoming tide. At night the air is pure crystal oxygen into the lungs.

Old Brendan Long of Dingle spoke of 'air currents'. Tommy Durkhan said that when the sun went down in clouds over Lettermore Hill, it would rain tomorrow; and so far has proved right. In the sodden west the low clouds constantly discharge rain onto the land, swans are up-ended in the small tarns that become lapis lazuli before stupendous sundowns, created by God or the moisture-laden Atlantic seaboard air.

There is a wren at the door. The place is cold but wholesome. There is a young bird on the water. The man is generous. God is generous. Una is well. The hound is young. The well is clean. Leave a big stool at the door. (*Simple Lessons in Irish*.) Wishing to be well; not exactly ill. Wishing to be ill, when not exactly well. Fog and mist mixed, darkening, and as far out as the wind that dried *your* first shirt.

181

Now, framed eerily in the small inset window, a greenish face appears behind rain-bespattered glass, under a greenish pork-pie hat at least one size too small for the head, and long-suffering greyish eyes look sorrowfully into the early morning obscurity of the odorous bedroom where the hessian-covered wall by the bed-head hides the stains caused nightly by the previous owner, a bachelor farmer, in violent projectile vomiting of Guinness over an unknown period of time. The window is open a foot, the morning cold comes in. A fine rain falls like some distress of the viscera.

'Your brother!'

We had arranged to meet by the bridge. The Morris Minor needed attention from the part-time mechanic who worked below the bridge in a graveyard of rusty car-parts. A pig named Emily was eating cow dung. Scraping with his fingernail on the glass, greenish tinged, my brother was so kind as to inform me that one of the cows was bleeding from an udder. I saw the sad profile, the unfortunate sodden headgear; a rain-drip depended from the narrow ill-coloured nose. Under one arm he carried a roof-slate. Behind him the needles of rain.

Well as a matter of plain fact I had no intention of even venturing out. The rain was slanting in against the thatch, the Maamturks had quietly betaken themselves elsewhere, with flocks of sheep reduced to the size of lice on their flanks. In the sodden west the overhang of clouds was once again leaking rain. Am I or am I not the same person whom I have always taken myself to be? A hundred times no. Brother C. had as a child a fancy to be a bird, a crow say. We had tamed a jackdaw, converted a biscuit tin into a bird-bath, and in this the fastidious creature bathed daily. Now the rats were frolicking at night in the kitchen, until one big buck rat electrocuted itself in the fridge. The stench beggars description. They were carousing on the dregs behind An Hooker, sole owner and proprietor, Johnny O'Toole, a man with an acid tongue, when he cared to use it.

* * *

Gas in the Decompression Chamber

The Mental Health Week in Ireland would end, as per advertised programme, at the Great Southern Hotel in Galway, with a Medical Ball. Charlie ('Hot Lips') Haughey, Minister for Health and Social Welfare, would attend. By a chain of accidents I found myself in the thick of it, having dined that night in the Claddagh Grill on the sixth floor, with a view of Galway Bay through the steamed-up bay window. Some Americans were dining there. Warm white wine, poor service, tasteless fish fresh from the bay, stained table-cloth, the tally not cheap. I went down in the lift and found them gathering below, the medical clan, the wives and sisters and friends. Below the bust of a cantankerous Roderick O'Connor in the lobby the typed notice was up.

DEPARTMENT OF ANAESTHETIC
HYPERBOLIC UNIT

A demonstration of the Decompression Chamber would be held, God willing, at 10 a.m. on Saturday October 22nd. Recompression (*sic*) Chamber.

By midnight the lone diner who had polished off his dinner with an Irish coffee (*de rigueur* for the *arriviste*) was thoughtfully blowing his nose into a large clean linen handkerchief under the clock in the lobby, Paddy in hand, confused by the hubbub of the medical convention now in full assembly. The excited wives, smoking like paddle-steamers, were getting into their stride. The bearded bust of the patriot O'Connor thoughtfully studied the carpet design, two harps emblazoned on a field of green. Wined and dined elsewhere the wives were already in great form. A serious father carried his small son, in pyjamas, up to bed. A group of merrymakers were flabbergasted to run into a group of friends.

'Patcheen!'

'Hairy!'

'Aw Jaysus.'

'Dja'know Petchunia?'

Observe the provincial social mill, Irish among Irish, all friends here.

'Vinnie, ary a goen up*steers*?'

'Whass up*steers*?'

'Dancen.'

Sober men smoking Sherlock Holmes pipes occupy the lounge, amid the gilt and green. The ice will give out long before midnight. Constricted about the hip and bust in Hellenic-style ball-gowns that expose white backs and arms, the wives appear to be in a perpetual froth of excitement, riggish charmers, knowing the minister to be there; rushing from lift to lobby, from bar to lounge, they might just run into him. (But someone was already having a word in his ear; the hooded ophthalmic eyes, vote-catching eyes, looked elsewhere, the head angled to receive a confidence.) Never trust a man with double vents. An employee in green uniform carried a zinc bucket past.

'God forgive me, that's all I'll say.'

'There's no sparks in my lighter!'

The country doctors, no strangers to women in distress, imperturbable men well accustomed to visiting ladies' bedrooms, pass nonchalantly from foyer to bar, or from bar to lounge, ball of malt in hand. Later a glass in *either* hand. Bareback ladies in geranium and raspberry chiffon, with great shoulders white as statuary, faces flushed with spirits and high excitement, take up strategic positions. The minister (smaller than imagined, dapper as George Raft) would surely pass. He was a ladies' man.

Male hotel employees whisper to female employees in green as they pass into a darkened dining-room. A backless strawberry chiffon speaks to a grass chiffon (monumental). Men in dinner-jackets walk on the balls of their feet. Green and raspberry chiffon mingle with the mauve and cowslip yellow (a mistake with orange hair), one lady carrying what appears to be a bicycle pump.

'Dermot Kelly – Ann Seymour.'

'Would you like a glass of something? . . . a glass of orange or something?'

An old-style hooded pram, with a baby asleep in it, is pushed from the lift at 1.45 a.m., well past a baby's bedtime. The reception lounge is emptying. Roderick O'Connor stares down morosely on emblazoned harps. Chiffon and escorts begin to ascend a long flight of stairs leading to the ballroom above. A buxom wife with fur draped across two-tone off-green hurries through, all business, after the manner of Garbo striding to the elevator in *Grand Hotel*, preceded by bellhops bearing floral tributes. An employee in morning-blue jacket and black trousers with razor creases carries through a full bucket of water. The doctor with the Don Ameche moustache who had not moved all night, wedged between chiffon and chiffon, is *still* drinking vodka and orange. A red bow tie meets a suavely affable priest. The great bulk of the faithful are ineffable. The hooded pram is pushed into the darkened dining-room. The last of the dancers have disappeared up the ascent. Frisky music issues thinly from the ballroom. Since ten past midnight, when the minister, summoned by an aide from without (someone was whispering in his ear again), had departed unobtrusively for Inishvickillane, the Medical Ball has been gathering momentum.

'Don't *attempt* to go, Eugene!'

'Second row? Ho-ho-ho!'

'Second row for *Ireland*.'

'Aw Jaysus.'

Lobby and lounge are emptying. The women rock on their high heels as though tormented. Room 133 is flooded. A foreign-looking beauty with brown back and fine shoulders is twisting her hips on the sofa, adopting dangerous Theda Bara poses. The Irish-coffee man, still alone, is downing short ones.

'It's never happened to me.'

'He was with you an Tony.'

'The last dance or was it the first?'

'You haven't seen my Kathleen have you?'

'Nooooo . . .'

'I'm interested in all Kathleens but my own Kathleen
would do.'

A heavy wife has capsized onto an empty sofa and seems
in need of air. It's her room that's flooded. A fubsy widow
stands before her. 'My room's flooded as well.'

'No!'

'I'll go straight up.'

'You'll do no such thing.'

The spoilsport with legs outstretched is fit to be tied; her
complexion high, this has happened before.

Ah, Galway.

The town was founded by the de Burghs in the thir-
teenth century. In 1498 the curfew was introduced. In
1641 the townspeople were all English. Lord Mayor Richard Brown assured Bingham the governor of Connacht
that the loyal citizens would 'untill the last gasp sustayne
all miseries and distresses' to defend it. Cromwell's dragoons stabled their horses in the empty houses. The Plantation was arranged by ghosts. Rent had always been high
there.

'He told me he was interested in buying a house. I told
him no way, there wasn't a chance.'

'How about you an me haven lunch?'

'White socks?'

A press photographer, a seedy Dick Crossman who had
arrived late and half cut, is now carefully arranging a group
of smirking ladies and laughing gentlemen against a wall,
for a commemorative group photograph. Though none are
sober, male hands are careful not to touch bare female
flesh. Four pints of Harp are carried through by two stout
drinkers, frowning.

'We're dyen to see the dance.'

'Is Hilary there?'

'You're crooked.'

'Andy will sort ye out.'

'Mebbe.'

'No maybe about it.'

The ball is ending, the reception desk empty, the hotel

staff gone home. It's difficult to get a drink. Mad Meg Magee has arrived, a mighty figure of flushed outrage, come late from some brisk business in Kells. The head waiter is in a huff and refusing to take orders. The bar seems to have been squirted with water. The barmen look as if they have been wrestling, the place deserted but for the usual last carousers, deep in some argument concerning horses. Lobby and Lounge are slowly emptying. From an armchair a lady in astonishing electric blue wishes to discuss amateur drama with me. She comes from Nenagh (opening wide her basilisk eye). Nenagh, haunt of dreams!

It's raining in Eyre Square as if it would rain there forever. In the old days the gypsies fought. In O'Flaherty's B & B, where the Aranmen stay, the beds are hard as penance. The pickpockets too have gone home. Glistening blackly two powerful cannons point at the ivy frontage of the Galway branch of the Bank of Ireland, the handsomest in the land.

'Oh dear God, it's spillen out of the heavens!'

'See you next year.'

'Be good now.'

Past Customs

1976

'Home is where one sets off from' – or words to that effect – homeward bound again after so long, aboard the SS *Avalon*. How distinctly unnerving to be among one's own again.

Collapsed toilets in Rosslare harbour. A complete stranger who seemed to know me said he would have slept in the open but feared being gored by a bull. Do bulls see at night?

Forgotten halts: Gorey, Ferns, Arklow. Shabby rolling-stock running under a harvest moon. People talking, talking. A single fellow whistling. The woman who loves Septembers; a youth who thought it a bad time for wasps. Freckled children chewing boiled sweets. The laughter of young daughters. 'She was havin' kittens.'

Dublin again, its nipping and eager airs. Persons and places, old pubs, missing, dug up, dead, vanished. One drowned by accident in the Atlantic, a suicide in Greystones, another gone to Canada to do it there. The incurable shabbiness of the capital; its old apathy replaced by something harder. House-breaking on the increase, offences against property with violence up twenty per cent already on last year, to keep pace with the maddened world, a brawly manner replacing older gentleness, when beards were baaed at by the children.

Fanagan the undertaker's dark limousine waiting with flowers for *defunctos* in damp Aungier Street. Ruddy-faced citydwellers back from the west where day never ends and all are happy as sprats. The English elm-blight strikes at Muckross, and a traffic jam extends from Bray Head to Donnybrook and on into An Lár.

Poor Dublin remains poor, the destitute drunks around

Mercer's Hospital, a new spleen in the graffiti, now gone all political. A taxi driver says trade is getting rougher; fish-netting protecting an optician's interior display from its own customers, just off Grafton Street. Few of the public clocks agree. Lawlessness on the rise. People offering cigarettes around in bars as in Spain. Would you prefer to be nearly drowned or nearly saved?

Flocks of magpies, and civic guards, on Palmerston Road, where Garret FitzGerald lives. The burglar-alarm business booming; broken shop windows and car glass everywhere. Fifty per cent of school-leavers jobless, but fivers and tenners flashed more than before in the bars that seem emptier, sadder. The jig-tune of the penny-whistler in the Green Arcade reminding one, in case one needed reminding, that the Irish are both shifty and merry. The venom of one side ('To hell with the Pope!') matched by the venom of the other ('Fuck the Queen!'), an accident-ward aseptic tinge prevails.

Query: can acetified cider go off in the freezer? Can drinking vinegar kill? Quite possibly, if taken in large enough doses. And why is it always raining in Wicklow Street?

The large cat, and the small snug, gone from the International Bar, though Our Boys school outfitters still stands opposite; in another life I was suitably kitted out there for misery in boarding-school.

'There's no such colour as black,' comes a voice from Smith's public bar on the canal, 'dark grey is the only colour you can see.' Such tactical opening gambits tend to suggest how perishable is our human lot, our time on earth.

'You'd be *amazed* . . . !'

Insecure good nature much in evidence. 'I'll give you a good one though . . .' WINDS PLAY HAVOC WITH SAILINGS. Will I ever get away?

Smell of turf-smoke in Celbridge. Pernod in the Castletown Inn, served not by a curate but by a spoiled priest, or so he said. My own ghost running around, hiding, miserable and elated at the same time. Friesian cattle at descant song in Springfield land. An Aer Lingus pilot's briefcase waits in the driveway. It's 8.30 a.m. and I have never left home.

Dublin Bay said to be polluted, a swimmer ingested a human turd in the forty foot one bright morning. Incidence of lost or murdered girls a sadly repetitive motif in a country allegedly at peace, among a people reputedly kind. Look again. Crime is unknown on St Helena, an islander once boasted to me.

'I must tell you another one . . . This one didn't happen to me though.'

A stout fellow like the sinister detective in Rom's movie *The Ghost that Never Returned* turns to me in the Bailey Bar to ask what day is it. A crack in the ceiling. Barman with a neck-brace. The ghost of a Gate actor moves along Merrion Square with the aid of a stick. *The Seagull* running at the old Gate. Dublin theatre as stuffy as ever: the creaking of ancient corsets. Maureen Potter goes on for ever, follies of King Street South.

Large seagulls stalk across Castle Street as if they owned the place. The people, the people, the nipping and eager air. We're near the sea; smell it. What day is it? Where am I at all?

Round Trip

1977

Heathrow and incoming Aer Lingus jet disgorging air passengers, slow-moving lines extruded from front and rear exit out onto the blackened tarmac. Huge humpbacked South African jets idling on the runway.

Aboard: incomprehensible Gaelic followed by no less incomprehensible free translation from cheery air hostess in mismatching pastel shades of green and blue and an unfortunate cap, which is removed as soon as possible. Approaches to Ireland always begin with linguistic riddles.

Two hostesses (now capless) pushing a drinks trolley. My flight companion knitting for dear life, but before you can say knit-one-purl-two Bull Island appears below, a line of brown objects straddling the shore. Bracing region of sea winds, shanks and divots, lost Dunlops, joybells (inaudible) of gay Malahide.

Dublin Airport in late July. Davy Byrne's half empty, as if I had never left. The casually intense manner of conversation resumed by habitually heavy smokers, students of human foibles; button-holers.

Missing: Theatre Royal, Regal Rooms Cinema, Capital and Metropole, Grafton Picture House, Mr Shakespear with golf umbrella. Shell of Moira Hotel. Combridge's subsumed into Brown Thomas. The hand-cut HB ice-cream replaced by chilled dog-biscuit covered in chocolate.

Constants: Jack Cruise at the Olympia. The International Bar in Wicklow Street (less its cat) and a chance encounter of two long-lost friends after twenty years, neither changed a whit, they swear: beads of sweat on nostrils induced by balls of malt. The heavy woodwork, elements of chance, old-style grey bags and tweed jackets from time of rationing, demob suits.

197

Toner's. Searson's snug on Portobello Bridge. The quest. Long-nosed paperseller from the past who had a pitch outside Combridge's corner, covering the Bailey and Davy Byrne's, walking as in a dream by Toner's in heavy overcoat, eyes blasted not by dreams but by the onrushing by-and-by.

Novelty: female bare backs and plunging *décolletage*.

Constants: in the sudden heat of July, with temperatures risen into the eighties, a man dies in the Meath Hospital. Pus coming from neck sore, the heavy smoker consoles the dumpy woman in heavy green overcoat. Smell of the Coombe, wail of the bereaved. Who will tell the widow? The Dublin poor. Set face on the stretcher. The short-tempered nurse, clang of the Emergency door.

Newness: Mansion House with new coat of white paint. Painted doors, no longer all green, and façades of a city in process of transforming itself.

Stephen's Green. The head park keeper breaking in assistant in brown uniform, armband. A face I remember. Much given to whistle-blowing, cane-brandishing, poses of rigid disappproval. (Whose grass is it anyway?) Manner of German gallery guards. Dating from days of Gardai with truncheons, Christian Brothers with sticks.

Oddity: well-designed rustic wooden tables and chairs near the playground. Replicas seen later in lay-by near Wicklow pine wood. Bavarian.

The last pawnbroker: Gorman of Cuffe Street.

Cut grass verges of Grand Canal cleared of weeds. Two houses side by side on Appian Way painted orange and shellac white. Ely House seen from Hume Street, in rose and terracotta, white woodwork. Georgian windows, the geometric flux, offset against the clouds.

'A glass of Jameson for the gentleman who just came in.'

As newspapers die elsewhere, bedevilled by unions, rising production costs, new ones start up in Ireland like the proverbial mushroom: the *Western Journal, What's On in Dublin, Hibernia Fortnightly Review* goes weekly.

* * *

A low-murmured 'What time is it at all?' heard outside Kevin Street public library; a poor female with chin and upper lip covered in white stubble. The thinker with ravaged brow paces around the pillar at Dwyer's lounge in Lower Leeson Street, plunged in reverie.

'Give it half an hour each way.'

Influx of young Spaniards. City of gulls, gusty skies. Slingback shoes producing the tensed female calf, buttocks thrown (not always happily) into prominence. Ice-cream addicts. Impromptu handball against dead-end walls.

'Where's the Princes' Bar gone to?'

'It's in oblivion.'

'How come?'

'You've come four years too late.'

Dead inward-looking buildings: Texaco House, Irish Life on Wellington Road, the Bank of Ireland branch at Ballsbridge. Inward-looking Ireland.

Pregnant women, as always; itinerants on Dawson Street, mute begging. Orange hair, antiques, arthritic septuagenarians on sticks, lost countrypeople.

Donycomper auction in Kildare. Heavy fixtures and fittings best suited to a Scots baronial way of living in cold northern clime. Heavy sets of dinner-plates, a plenitude of glass and coffee cups; oppressive grand living that would require an army of servants to support. Small beautiful bedrooms above. Major Kilpatrick.

New factory alongside the old cemetery at Donycomper, producing odd effect, like blasphemy from a priest. The bridge at Celbridge, the National School closed. Straffan: Christ with one hand off, before crucifixion, among polychrome Stations. Lovely reaches of Liffey below the bridge, mansions of the rich among the trees, raining in Kildare.

Over the hills into a dry Co. Wicklow. Bray: airless lounges, piped music in what used to be the Royal Hotel. Tongue-tied girls in the company of bowsies. In the main street, bursting denims replacing Bloom's dream of well-filled hose. Stench of cigars. First, second finger and thumb of right hand stained to knuckle-joint by nicotine: effect of iodine swab, or dipped in cowshit.

Dun Laoghaire: the rebuilt church with blind walls. West Berlin style of shopping complex. Bulloch harbour full of pleasure craft, flags of two yacht clubs blowing. As Greystones harbour. Crowds on the sea-front, charms of Sandycove with its low skyline, Virginia creeper.

Walk over Bray Head to Greystones, breakfast in the Copper Kettle. Girls on ponies, high hedges, 'Protestant beech', Ronnie Drew, always giving the impression he should be somewhere else.

As the Korchnoi–Polugayevsky chess game, after nineteen moves, ended in a draw at Evian in France, a trip to the west. Scene of a murder: Castlebar.

Kingsbridge Station now become Sean Heuston, pleasantly transformed from my days of grim departures for boarding-school. Castlebar in the evening. Rowdies along main street. Small man with blazing ears in cramped bar, speaking passionately about greenfly. 'They do be watching you from the ivy.'

Two white-haired sisters like hens on a perch, main street under constant observation from window; disappear into dark recess at rear for tonic water. Pontoon: the Lake of the Blind Trout. 'The horses are leppin' around. They have no heat. They'd madden you.'

Overcast at midday, smoke from a chimney, sound of whetstone on scythe blade, sheep coming over the hill, swallows on the telegraph wires. Empty fields, shells of cottages, circular skies over Mayo, wheeling, a lark, a hare bounding away, trout rising in the little lake where we swam. 'On a calm evenin' you do see them leppin', says Bridget McHale. Echoes of Synge: the widow Quinn.

Healy's Hotel on Lake Corrib. Nose-to-nose conversation at bar, cloth caps touch, peeling noses. The huge pike in the glass case seems to be listening. 'We were at hay all day.'

'The world is a mode of the Divine exaltation and every sane fragment of force ends in a fertile passion that is filled with joy' (Synge). Fever speaking: TB. An Irish Kafka? The tremor of excitement. Poteen: a shock of joy in the blood.

Cycling downhill into the western pseudo-dark, listening to the cuckoo, a Mayo wall surmounted with barbed wire rose up and hit me, poteen-powered, head on. The stars, the wheeling sky. Synge saw two eyes observing him from a clump of trees in a clearing.

The bay of green delirium.

'A human being finds a resting place only when he is in harmony with his surroundings, and is reminded that his soul and the soul of nature are of the same organization.'

'It is the infertile excitements that are filled with death.' Soho strip-shows, porno movies?

Mayo: natures profoundly emotional from the beginning. The bog road of irregular stone, the overwhelming sky. The universe as the Divine unconscious. 'Is not a twilight as vital as a human mood?' Synge wrote in *Under Ether*, in December 1897.

A small man sipping Jameson in McEnery's at Foxford advises me to look for education in the Bowry. He ran a taxi there. A large pair of crutches by him. Skid Row he knew. Small lame baffled man, his bedroom a back room filled with tins, shop stock.

Reeling skies, the hare on the hill, the hedge ablaze. Fianna Fáil sponsored dance in Pontoon dance hall, the only ugly building thereabouts. The three-star hotel: low-voiced ordering in almost religious gloom, a minute helping of salmon fresh from Lake Corrib. French fishermen departing next morning with hotel hampers.

Horses on the road. Absolute silence of the nights. The five empty villages. Ghosts of schoolchildren yelling and screeching on the road. The broad-shouldered ladies in print frocks give low-voiced orders.

Dublin again. *Irish Times*: letters to the editor concerning a malicious review. Press photo of female cricketer's frillies stirring up correspondence.

Charms of the city: absence of sex magazines in news-agents and in kiosks, as in London, West Berlin, Amsterdam, less so in sinful Paris, thanks to Madame Pom.

Palmerston Park, a region of magpies, civic guards; a man reading *Hibernia* in a parked car. Ineffable sadness of pillarboxes, once red now green; telephone kiosks too, absolute conveyors of bad news. The name SALLINS seen from a train window on a darkening day; the name ATHY. My past.

Trip to Kilkenny. Sean Heuston Station again. 'Poor Shamus is dartin' back.' Train windows (by British Rail) never to open, air-conditioning that doesn't work, a dauntingly restricted bar. Inchicore sidings transformed by lawns. Kildare, Athy, Carlow, Thomastown. Kilkenny wheatfields. Last beautiful buildings on a small scale: the lovely wayside granite stations. Thomastown. Protestant architecture, Catholic stone-masons. Old advertisements on sheets of tin, the jolly hand-waving Raleigh cyclist. Kincora Plug. Old shop façades: Murphy the butcher, a cobbler.

Horse-flies savage as Russian wasps; slate-blue of Blackstairs Mountains; fields of ripening wheat before them; above, massed cumulus. But soon back to plebeian earth, with artificial flowers and large toy tricolour on dashboard of new Fiat parked outside ugly modern house of conforming Corporation ugliness, and a powerfully built young mother with baby in minute lawn dominated by electric mower. Bridge House pub across the Nore facing an abbatoir, a pipe pouring blood into the river.

An evening of limpid blueness and peace in the hunting lodge, trees all afflicted with some fungoid disease; the path through the overgrown garden, the field of barley bounded by a dark pine plantation; slate-blue of distant hills, serenity. County of champion hurlers and priests, ghost of Parnell. The Pricketts.

A low ten-arch bridge at Inistioge, 'anciently called Grenan', of the Irish Bally-Mac-Andon, signifying Fitz-Anthony's town. The old bridge, then of five arches, built in 1792. The Augustinian monastery, the Spotted Dog, the monument in the square to the Brownsfoords. A village very English in style, still colonized by English woodworkers, pine-strippers.

Round Trip

The Curragh. Newbridge, Sallins, all disappear. Darkening on an August Bank Holiday threatening rain; night and rain coming. Train window shattered by stone thrown from embankment, announcing Dublin again; Simon and Garfunkel playing on transistor, smell of sulphur, taxis in a line by the station.

'In a little time places may begin to seem the only hieroglyphs that cannot be forgotten' (Yeats). Too true. A round tower, a path worn across a field by cattle, a standing stone. Wake up in golden sunshine. My past. Yours, too. Go on.

Loose Chippings

1977

Away from the glutted cities! Kildare: a county of two moods, wet and dry. Somnolent, woody. The flat unaccentuated accent of Middle Ireland. Dis, dat and de udder ting. An' de mudder to boot.

Friesian cattle, nurses in sanatorium grounds by the Liffey. 'Oh look, Mammy, he'll be in the wather!' Lucan. The dying beech tree two hundred years old in Springfield meadow, the eucalyptus tree in the yard where yellow roses climb against the stable walls. Miss Victoria Campbell.

Gone: the tall two-storey gate-lodge at Killadoon, the pitched gable roof, the mullioned windows, the wooden porch now a pile of rubble, the Hollingsworth family gone. The old gateway gone too. Lord Leitrim once passed here.

Boy in wellingtons, gloves, front tooth missing, pulling poisoned dockweed. Swim in the Liffey. Drag of the current, dragonflies skimming, slate-grey shit of geese along the bank, nettle-beds; a grey squirrel among beech saplings. The acorn-covered path by the river, hum of teeming nature, Killadoon House with its twenty-four windows back among trees. Gone: Springfield orchard.

'Emer, where's the kay?'

DUBLIN: the banjaxed legs of Dublin working women. St Stephen's Green in late evening August sun, walkers outlined in gold, as if underwater. The city in the grip of God.

The spare-time gardener, a Belfastman, in O'Neill's of Suffolk Street, with Veronica Complex: 'What have they done to my Lord?' Quoting St Augustine. 'The hot cities of life.' Singing quietly into his pint.

Palace Bar, Fleet Street.

'By Jaysus, I'm tired. I wanta go home.'

'Tired is it? Go home is it? Weren't the Jairmans carryin' packs as big as dimselves, an' dey oney skeletons!'

Sean Heuston Station. Departure fever. The young one in frilly skirt twirling herself on platform 5, showing white thighs, white knickers. The aged traveller with Tolstoyan beard; a young Franciscan monk with orange hair like Rasputin. A stout peroxided lady with shaky head looking down at the tracks. The tannoy!

'Will Imelda Lurcan please go to the kip-house.'

The crowded bar, agitation of the travellers.

'The train now standing on platform *wun* leaves for Tralee thirteen-fifteen!'

The half-empty miserable bar.

'Will Imelda Lurcan please go to the ticket orifice.'

Card-playing, orange-eating, Lucozade-swigging travellers racketing through Kildare. 'Give us a blast of Neil Diamond.' Two gigantic officials in splendid uniforms like admirals of the rail, the congested bar. Outside, stratocumulus floating below mackerel skies in washed-out cobalt above Kildare. All the church spires of Ireland are the same. May you be in Heaven half an hour before the Devil knows you are dead.

Loose crimplene tops worn over bras and skintight bluejeans over bikini panties; pastel shades favoured. Extraordinary quiet entry into Killarney in the evening. Mute greetings and embraces on the platform, travellers and welcomers as if in a trance. Three Dublin cowboys in outsize Mexican hats waving to our train, now pulling out backwards.

TRA LI

FEARANN FUAR

TRA LI. Line of red-and-white single-decker buses, sophisticated nuns driving off in a white Ford Cortina upholstered in imitation leopardskin. Bite of the Atlantic. Hitchhiking to Dingle. Trio of unremittingly foul-mouthed youths encountered in Ashe's wayside bar. The *deux-chevaux* ('The

Blue Lagoon') driven at breakneck speed. Badmouthing womankind, foreigners, 'Brits', with particular venom against Americans ('Yankees'), Germans preferred. Hating Dingle, work; all on the make, all on the dole, Provo bait.

Dingle by night: a sort of Irish Torre de Mar on the Atlantic, less bikinis and stench of drains. Sole on the bone at The Armada, chilled Bordeaux. The tourist-infested town. The Spanish Cellar, a closed boat-yard, two sixty-foot trawlers under construction on the ways, costing £200,000 each, built in six months by forty men. Old drawings on unwanted postcards show Dingle Bay full of trawlers.

'She was locked last night.'

'She takes a drink. Oh begod she does.'

'She looks to be in a trance.'

'Oh Jaysus, she's livin' far away.'

'She's lookin' *desperate*.'

'Mind you *he* could let down a few.'

'He didn't know his own strength.'

The boat that sank like a basket in the harbour of the Red Ox. Wailing Foal Rock, Eagle Mountain: Danish animism in Gaelic names. The Spanish Cellar, trade in the Middle Ages. Antiquity of Dingle. A lesson in Spanish history from Patrick Crohansberry in Long's Bar. Two harmonicas disposed in deep pockets, a long American mouth-organ. The Croppy Boy played in jazz time. *A-tisket-a-tasket*. 'Ah Jaysus, I do love Ella.' A Negro voice singing in the gloom. 'I'm a whore for jazz.'

History made to sound like a family feud. How he downfaced the Harvard professor. His history maybe culled from *Reader's Digest*. His father through the Dardanelles, Gallipoli, the Somme, did not know the meaning of fear. They couldn't kill him.

New Ireland with its blind-view architecture: Scelig Hotel, Grade A, a cross between a motorway diner and small airport lounge; an unfortunately sited car park. A mother speaking in hushed tones before a George Campbell

canvas, her two daughters fidgeting. Heavy Germans heading in a purposeful way to the dining-room. Sabina and
Conor playing pool with French boys in the playroom. An
orange helicopter air-lifting roof material to the intrepid
Haughey's island hideout on Inishvickallane.

'He's mad in the right way.'

Stills from *Ryan's Daughter*, all in faked sepia. Lies about
Ireland put out by Ford in *The Quiet Man* were swallowed
by the French then; myths told by Lean about Kerry
swallowed by Germans and Scandinavians now.

'A proper holiday is sittin' on your arse in front of
television.'

Lord Ventry's country seat seen across the bar. Now in
possession of Sisters of Mercy. Three woeful traditions
combined in one closed institution. Claustrophobia of
Catholic convents; the death-pale statuary, austerity of the
dormitories, his lordship's gunroom. Ogham stones along
the drive, a young novice sunning herself. Land and estate
bought and sold in different ways; a grant for Cromwell's
butcher, backed by Scots' inheritance, now perpetuated by
the Sisters of Mercy.

The pale clouds come to rest on the mountains, the
exhausted clouds over Kerry. Brandon Head, the races
washed out, £700 down the drain. Foreign semi-nude
cyclists on the by-roads, bloody cloven hooves at sharp
corners, an abattoir truck shedding its messy load. Ventry
(the Fair Strand), site of a great battle in ancient times, in
the days of boulder-throwing giants. Bottle-hurling and
arson still persists in the North, old ways dying hard,
history attempting to repeat itself with pygmies.

In 1585, in the twenty-eighth year of her reign, Elizabeth
I granted a charter to Dignenacush and a royal stipend of
£300 to build a town wall. The remains are of clay and
very thick. Elizabeth II, looking pale and wan in the
twenty-fifth year of *her* reign, spoke of goodwill and
coming peace from Coleraine University. Seed of the
Goddess.

A flat Limerick voice relapsing into Gaelic, where everything said begins to sound like a grievance. The dull female servant with huge varicose veins who answered the convent bell summoned a nun to show us around, the pale hand gliding along the banister after dust.

In Kruger's Bar in Dunquin a parchment-pale old cleaning-woman is tidying up. A Bloody Mary on the wall outside, the Blaskets obscured by nettles beyond the cow-dungy yard. The blind eyes and orange hair of the assassinated President Kennedy embroidered against images of White House, Capitol, Old Glory hoisted on the masthead.

'Paddy, I'm over here!'

At a campsite a couple are watching Haughey's roofing materials being lifted over to the island, the last run, the sun sinking, the little slip darkening. American potters play frisbee in an upland field, the day's work over. A bronzed blonde in shorts is sipping Guinness in Kruger's yard. Children moan in the gloomy bar. 'Be a good boy an' play with your rattle.' A Northern voice in the gloom orders Bacardi and gin. Huge Germans with becalmed faces are leaving, wearing shorts. A brown foam of Guinness like sores on lips.

Ridges of a defunct tillage marked in steep weals athwart the hill. Heavy-lidded eyes of a bearded drinker. Ice-cream dispenser with bunches of bananas on top, odd to see in a bar. In Loving Memory of Maurice (Kruger) Kavanagh, by his US Friends; the marble plaque is behind glass. I hear harp music, mixed with turf-smoke equally dense. Patriotic humours. In the Computer Centre a lone darts-player plays a game against himself. Bob Quinn's *Cloch* (stones) is showing at the local. Donkeys braying in the Dunquin dark.

SLEA HEAD on a blue August day. Froth of the Atlantic rim, green on the Ballyferriter side, with motionless cormorants on a rock. The divers dropping vertically. Balmy south-west wind, bees in the gorse, white clouds drifting above this treeless headland. No flies, only Haughey's orange

helicopter making one more inward trip over Inishnabro.
A fellow playing a penny-whistle near a fearful drop.

KILLORGLIN on the Laune. First day of Puck Fair. Light
variable winds forecast, warm away from parts affected by
onshore winds. Your first time? There's a treat in store for
you, but mind your wallet. Killorglin crammed with drop-
outs, punk rocker with imitation razor blades worn about
the neck. A reader of tarot cards with an inverted question
mark printed on his forehead. Some German girls causing
a stir.

'Do you live here do you? *On* the bridge? *Under* the
bridge? When the tide comes in the water comes up. *Beside*
the bridge?'

'Is your friend a dummy?'

The authentic Voice of Kerry: 'Don't mind that.' The
Fermoy fife and drum band belting out 'A Nation Once
Again' outside Sheehy's Bar (Pub Grub). A welt on the
drum and up the main street with them, stepping it out to
the strains of 'The Minstrel Boy'.

The horse-fair, the horse-fair! Tenners crackling in rapid
transactions, £270 changing hands. On the platform, a
strapping wench in pale blue briefs, the backs of her thighs
reddened by back-kicks, dancing in black pumps, stiff-
faced. Smartly dressed girleens in short cloaks jigging away.
The barkers are becoming hoarse.

'Have anudder go – the yella wan!'

Not a man sober, one bare from the waist up. Garbage
cans overflowing by midday, also a reveller outside
McGillycuddy's Foodstore who cannot stand on his own
feet, the street tilting. A line of Kerry girls sit with their
lads on the bridge wall.

'Dim tints, summa dim are oney rite for a day.'

Face of John Lennon under Afro haircut peering from
window of passing coach. *Uilleann* pipes droning away like
maddened bees.

Arrival of King Puck, a black mountain goat with great
horn-span and colourless goat-eyes, winched up into a

platform where he can see all the goings-on, and fodder all hours. The Kerry compère makes jokes against Cork. The junk on the stalls is shabby: plastic holy-water fonts, Infants of Prague in glass bells, hourglasses, toy helicopters, miniature garden gnomes, St Martin de Porres prayer-books bound in moss-green, holy relics at 35p each. St Joseph in plastic, oil lamps, garden grottos, Gates of Heaven. Bawling brats, the turning wheel of fortune. 'Kiss Me Slowly; Squeeze Me Tight' printed boldly around the brim of a straw hat worn by a small boy. Help Kerry's mentally handicapped children. Two wild-eyed bearded men of Clare whisper urgently to me in praise of Scariff. 'You'd be lost there. You'd never find yourself there,' one says.

The other, looking wildly about him: 'You wouldn't know yourself in Scariff. *Nobody* in Scariff knows themselves.'

'That's the place for me.'

'Right so. You'll come with us then?'

The Furies, each with their torch on high. Houlihan in a purple shirt, the owner of King Puck himself. Ella Coffey. Maria Simmonds-Gooding. The last pubs emptying. Lines of fairy-lights suspended across the bridge. The last buses, the last coaches, the last revellers walking home.

KILLARNEY: the whore of Ireland. A region of bare midriffs. Bosoms begin under the armpits. Smell of chips and vinegar. The low awnings slapping. Carcasses of hoofless cattle being offloaded from a huge Killarney Meat Supply trailer packed to the roof with slaughtered kine. Germans in caravans passing through Kells. Soon we are tired of Killarney.

The impossibility explained to us in painstaking detail, of travelling *across* Ireland; either by hitching (difficult) or by bus (impossible). It was only possible to reach Kilkenny town by passing through Limerick; no worse destination. We decide to split the taxi fare.

The taxi journey to Thomastown (125 miles) on a series

Ronda Gorge & Other Precipices

of back roads and by-roads that went mauve and then grape-purple, as the day drew on, counting two stops for refreshment; going on through avenues of beech hedge, from Brandon Head on the Dingle peninsula to Brandon Hill in Kilkenny, via Rathmore, Millstreet, Mallow, Mitchelstown, Clogheen, Newcastle, Clonmel, Callan, Strongford, over the bridge to Thomastown.

Between the Mullagharetry, Ballyhoura, Galty and Slieveardah Hills to the north; the Derrynasaggart, Boggerah, Nagles, Knockmealdown and Slievenamon Hills to the south; down the Blackwater valley by ruined castles and orchards full of fruit. The Suir. Leidensdorf. Butchers in white standing at the gates of a canning factory.

To end up on a damp evening in Ben Hennessy's Jerpoint Inn in Thomastown. A voice repeating: 'Kultchur ... Kultchur.' A Lehár operetta on the radio. Birdscares going off in the wheatfield, in the night, in the rain.

'I hear she's blind.'

'Of *course* she's blind.'

'What do you tink?'

Back in Emor Street, the *pied-à-terre* off the South Circular Road, the cat is getting sick, the skipping-rope looped on the clothes-line, the clock stopped (its nerve broken). Go on.

A Crack in the Distributor Head*

1986

*An eightfold innuendo: *crack* (Irishism), great gas, unbridled merriment; *crack*, a blow, an attack; *crack on head*, Donnybrook Fair fight; *crack in head*, the ill-governed land; *cracked wall*, Ireland falling; *crack in distributor head*, malfunctioning engine, by implication 'modernized' Ireland; sex-maddened modern Ireland, *Kopflust*, Kathleen ni Houlihan grown sluttish; *crack* (vulgar), vulva, vagina.

Cuckoos have been seen but not heard. The swallows return in fewer numbers each spring, now that the barns are torn down. But daisies still come up in the eleven graveyards, one for paupers and a nice little one for the nuns. Some are closed, packed out, don't you know. The Bleeding Horse public house may reopen near Mullaghmast.

Résumé 1

To return again to childhood haunts is to retreat into a land that has become unreal and *hermetically* disturbing. A paler shade of grey prevails there. For such a lost soul as your correspondent, whelped nearly fifty years ago not thirty Irish miles away, Athy is best entered in the evening, privily viewed in the gloaming.

The living population (some 5,500 souls) seem stupefied, as if by some shock or wrong done to the collective psyche long ago.

A male hand passes me a note. I read in 'prentice backhand:

> *O'er the rath of Mullaghmast*
> *In the solemn midnight's blast*
> *What bleeding spectres passed*
> *With their gashed breasts bare!*

The Pale-ground is of course as no other in the land, was and still is as a 'place or state of rest called Limbo'; for time has stopped here, on the south-west corner of Co. Kildare,

217

at more or less the limit where Irish decency could still survive.

A most grudging spring daylight shines here after the long foul winter and the people are pale as ghosts in late April, the time for Punchestown Races and the seventieth anniversary of the Easter Rising. The previous summer was the worst in living memory, and February the coldest since God knows when.

The Irish, being by nature a contrary lot, were always adept at pulling down whatever England had seen fit to erect on Irish soil – not excluding the capital – but, I ask you, how can a small town that has died *five times* up to the middle of the fifteenth century still be alive today? Miracles never cease.

As a loving mother may lavish special attention on an ailing child, so the still-unextinguishable *habitantes* of Athy love Athy, with its barley-malting silos, Tegral steel-rolling, in this hub of the barley-growing area with 1,100 unemployed. Borden of Canada is here, and so too is Klaus Schmidt in the catering trade, while young Bradbury owns the Leinster Arms Hotel as well as the bakery across the road.

I was shut out of my hotel room in the Leinster Arms one Sunday night after closing time. The tall receptionist had given me the wrong key. The place was deserted and the bar closed, the shutters down. Far away a figure appeared.

'What strange people we are.'

'How did the boxing go?'

'It went well.'

In Doyle's a small dumpy unsober woman was taking Paddy and lemonade and attempting to waylay stray males on their way to the shadowy Gents.

'The daffodils is droopin',' she tells me.

'I reared yiz all!' she calls to a male back flinching away.

'FF goes back to its roots,' claimed a sub-leader of the *Irish Press* in a thick provincial accent; but where else would FF go? Seasonal work is still available on the bog.

The Bog Allen is finished, but there is talk of extensive vegetable-growing in the rich bog soil. There is also talk of a facelift and coat of paint for the Leinster Arms. The coldest February preceded the wettest March and January was miserable; now in late April the Barrow is rising and the swallows still absent.

Pale spectres of warriors long dead stray by the muddy Barrow stream, cracking their finger-joints and cursing under their breath, waiting for the trout-rise, watching for poachers, or some sign of human life. Cattle are 'bawling with hunger' in the sodden fields, dying in a bovine famine. The evergreens are turning brown, the short grass decaying. If you knock down a swallow's nest the cows will milk blood.

The semi-deserted bars blare out tellynews augmented by transistors not always turned down. Two coloured boxers square up to each other on a silent screen. Cowboy Reagan squares up to Colonel Gaddafy not so silently, while Señora Safia gives the thumbs-up sign to photographers and swears vengeance on the US pilot who destroyed their home, killed a fifteen-month-old adopted daughter, in the air-strike sent out from England. Blame Thatcher too.

Résumé 2

Athy was originally Norman, a market town on the Kilcullen–Castlecomer road, the old highway from Dublin to the south; until it passed by marriage to the house of Kildare. Edward Bruce sacked it in 1307, the Irish themselves having had a go at it seven years previously.

In 1420 the Earl of Desmond did much slaughter to the terrible army of the O More at the Red Moor of Athy, the sun obligingly standing still for three hours in the heavens. It fell to Eoghan Rua O'Neill himself in 1645; to Oliver Cromwell's troops five years later.

Nothing much has happened since, until John Minihan

photographed the wake of Katy Tyrrell in 1977. He had studied the technique of Curtis who had recorded the decline of the North American Indians, another race deprived of their own land and rights, from 1896 to 1930. 'Death is the beginning,' wrote John fatalistically. The only Happy Hunting Grounds would exist in a recharged after-life, or in the Indian head itself.

> *At last thou heard the fearful wail*
> *That o'erloads the sullen gale . . .*

O'erloads? Anything for a bad rhyme, or a sullen quatrain

> *As the waning moon shines pale*
> *On the curs'd ground there.*

Curs'd? The usual quota of cornerboys snigger at junctions here, prop up the corners, catcall at out-of-town drivers, stare in a hostile fashion at strangers, that is to say, anybody not from hereabouts. There are two sides to Athy. An entrance *and* an exit?

The price of funerals has gone up. Some fifty years ago it might cost you £3 with pipe, tobacco and poteen thrown in. Now a slap-up funeral would cost you £1,000, with coffin, hearse and mutes.

'I had a busy day. Two funerals.'

'Shure *that's* only pleasure.'

Slagging (or 'messing') is a popular local pastime, as darts elsewhere. Even the station sign looks broken:

ATH I

But no more than Bradbu. Or no stranger than Ophthalmic Optician. Or Ann's Betting Place. The sniggering corner-boys jeer openly at cyclists who pass, dressed for winter, blue in the face on antiquated push-bikes, passing between the two bridges. The Barrow bridge is named Cromabu after the Fitzgerald war-cry; the Augustine bridge crosses the Grand Canal where no swans paddle, and a plaque above shows a monkey with a child in its arms.

Does Athy dream bad dreams?

The Annals of Athy ceased recording ages and ages ago.

There is of course a Provo bar. And the Hole in the Wall gang had *Gruppensex* with a minor in a graveyard, did time in the Joy. Rumour (the greatest of all whores) has it that the girl went willingly. The Club Inn is rocking with boredom. Two punters up (or down) for Punchestown Races are lashing into two well-tortured chickens covered in some kind of sauce and drinking nothing stronger than water in the dining-room of the Leinster Arms.

'Eat away there and give me a shout when you're ready.'

A group of habitual messers are enjoying convivial backchat, messing and slagging away in the snug at Bertie (RIP) Doyle's on Woodstock Street between the two bridges, known colloquially as *Sráid Choill an Chip'*, the Street of Rain in my time there. An old black-and-white photo shows a pulley and tripod hoisting a haycock onto a cart in pre-bogey days, in hilly Tinnahealy, Co. Wicklow.

The two coarse eaters are still stuffing it in. The Provo bar looks dead from outside, but you never can tell. *Supergrass* is showing at the Grove. The municipal baths crowded with excited kids. Articulated trucks squeeze by the Leinster Arms where the pretty and vivacious young Mrs Palmer won't stop gassing, with little daughter Claudine and mother Lil, in the lounge bar, stared at by a silent Kerryman who lives rough, and won't talk.

'Any sign of Anna?'

'Anna was at Mass.'

'On her own?'

'I couldn't say for sure.'

Outside, a thin fretting rain falls like penance, and as though it intended to rain forever. Laois (pronounced 'leash') have defeated Dublin, and the final in Croke Park will be a 'sea of blue and white', or so says a tellysportsman in a rhapsodic spurt of purple prose.

'I'd say it's down for the day.'

'Were you out last night – no?'

Young Michael Harrington is laying a £1 bet on Any Which Way to win, for an unseen punter glued to the tellyraces in the back bar of Doyle's, where the messing and slagging continue unbated.

'You have to more or less keep up with the times,' a cheery male voice says, 'or else fall behind.'

'It's freshenin' up a bit.'

The persistent rain falls at an angle on sodden Athy.

A pleasing novelty here (live population five and a half thousand still, give or take a few, dead population unknown) is that your pint-imbibers *do not read newspapers*. A behatted man with one enlarged glass eye stares critically into his pint, like an eagle coldly surveying the plains teeming with game.

The grey station looks closed-up as a prison. No trains will ever pass through ever again. I am here for life.

> *The man who drives an ambulance*
> *Is not engaged in fun . . .*

I read near the door at Doyle's pub. Lines penned by ex-ambulance-driver Des Keogh. Walter Hurley sprawls at the bar.

'The lowest form of life on God's earth!'

A flat unaccented accent suits the men of the Kildare plains. Here they cannot allow their hopes to rise too much. History has branded them as malcontents. Patriotism in this walled-in and hedged-off enclave has always been a melancholy matter; but then Irish nationalistic fervour has always been tinged with an ancestral sadness. Betrayers and informers hide behind every corner.

Now Julia Mahon, with two buckets of pigswill slung over the handlebars of her High Nelly, is off again to talk to her mother in St Michael's cemetery.

'It's freshenin' a bit outside.'

'Begod an' it's not.'

I am set upon near closing time in Doyle's by a small

malcontent who seems to be under the impression that he is in the very presence of the Arch Enemy (Mr George Henry Oliver Sassanach Esq. himself, with horns), waving a cigarette in my face, rocking on the soles of his shoes, intent on being offensive.

'Are you English or are you Irish?'

On his upper lip a growth of hay-coloured moustache. Shure that Noel Dunne fella wouldn't hurt a flea.

'Do you tell me that now. And where do you come from yourself?'

'*A ripa ulteriore*. From the further shore.'

Résumé 3

The cuckoo, pretty bird, should surely be heard, not seen? And even greyhounds will turn on you in your own back yard, having no sense of smell. Had not three such, two muzzled, all three in greyhound-jackets, fixed upon me their accusing stare opposite Ann's Betting Shop? And of course there are two sides to most things, including Athy. And what's it a sign of when you see a woman making off with a monkey in her arms?

'Welcome home, stranger!'

But soon I was passing through Co. Kilkenny where a fresher air was blowing over the land and the frisky Nore was flowing under splendid old stone bridges, the low Brandon Hills as ever a backdrop gliding by, Mount Leinster somewhere to the right and now receding, a hawk flying over a field, the cattle lying down or standing, incomprehensible announcements coming over the tannoy announcing stations in outer Patagonia, but soon we were pulling into Cill Choinnig and my journey over.

The Other Side

1983

I am in England. Everything tells me so. The sweet sound of an old violin sweeps over Ealing; here breathes authentic atmosphere. Land of the Welfare State, that chronic form of civil inertia; labour disputes, bad news, phone-in radio programmes, Capital Radio, Radio London. A Mr Dalgliesh of Slough on the line.

'All lines are now open.'

Dalgliesh (effusively): 'Ah, good evening gentlemen . . .'

'Get your priorities right.'

'I have a problem.'

At Sherwood Zoo, Nottingham, a Formosa deer died from a broken neck after crashing into a fence, a bison escaped, two flamingos were crippled, and two puma cubs were destroyed by their mother, because of low-flying Phantom jets from Hucknall Aerodrome. 'You cannot tell those boys what to do,' said an RAF spokesman.

At Errigton Close, Bolton, a young bellringer, Jane Hemingway, was swept to the belfry ceiling holding onto the rope yesterday, and then fell ten feet to the floor while practising with other bellringers.

James Finch, an Englishman accused in the Whisky a Go-Go murder case, delayed the hearing today by swallowing wire and biting off the top of his little finger, in Brisbane, Australia.

At Powerstock, West Dorset, died Mr Kenneth Allsop, aged fifty-three, of acute barbiturate intoxication.

* * *

Three men were apprehended and brought to court when suspicion fell on them because they were running with bated breath. All three were sentenced in a Leeds court. (Is it only because behaviour leaves no fossils that we are forced to search for it in bones and teeth?)

London: Oxford Street, a dirty river, a bazaar, poster photos of female posteriors suggesting sodomy and the birch. Cassette rock throbs from open doors, the Hare Krishna novices in orange smocks sport shaven polls. Double-decker buses elephantine in the defiles, bound for Marble Arch, Hackney, Morden, Land's End. Asphalt, petrol, Academy cinemas, the hump. The crowd being flushed down Regent Street.

NATURE GAS ERUPTION IMPERILS TOWN

Wassily Kandinsky at Lefevre gallery. An art of the inner eye near to music (these paintings look like scores for silent singers). Kandinsky, friend of Klee, was enamoured of circles and with what he termed the 'spiritual perfume' of the triangle. Arthur Rubinstein, too, referred to the 'perfumed' piano, a camouflaged percussion instrument. 'It has a link. You believe in it. Suddenly the piano begins to smell. Perfumed, you know.' (A Chopin nocturne.)

Thomas Edison had to rest his teeth on the piano in order to hear it play (vibrate); had not heard a bird sing since he was twelve years old.

To invent, you need imagination and a pile of junk. Writing is like shooting: complete stillness, the subject caught in the sights, the trigger squeezed.

On being tortured: hearing the cursed word from the cursed mouth. Urban trembling. The collective eye betrays

228

pain, anger, bewilderment. Crammed onto the pavements,
des gens heureux.

'The fuckin salt watah was leakin through.'
'When 'ees 'ad a few bee-ahs 'ee lykes a bitta aggro.'
'All lines are now open.'

Islington, Haringey, Kilburn, the long drag. Nodes. Thom.
Judd. Old Parr. The Angel, winos and turps-drinkers supine
on the green. Bakerloo Line, Swiss Cottage. A junkie in a
wall recess giving himself a fix at ten in the morning. Felt-
pen graffiti on the tiles:

> *Clap your hands*
> *Jump for joy*
> *Because Tony's going to kill Roy.*

When the clouds start to build up, walk across Primrose
Hill. The Gulf Oil man in his blue uniform is drinking in
the George IV on Rosslyn Hill.

Dinginess of the Strand. Stench of the river in Victoria
Embankment Gardens, a fanatic issuing dire threats on
behalf of the Catholic Evidence Guild. Ghosts of Salvation
Army band blaring away at ghost-music near de Barra's flat.

'That's it, Len. Come an sit down by me an do up your flies
an all.'
'The flames are yellow. Something comes into me fuckin
mind'.

Met a righteous citizen, another madman, off Hampstead
Heath; who pointed out a low-flying police helicopter
circling above the heath; since it was illegal to fly below a
certain altitude, he had a good mind to take his number,
he could see the pilot's face; some days previously the
fellow had landed, checking on suspected indecent expo-
sure, and found a woman breast-feeding her baby.

* * *

The Bird in Hand, down Friern Barnet way. The pubs of London are named after whore-houses (Aubrey). Strip-tease at Shepherd's Bush and on the Old Kent Road.

'When I get 'errings I do 'em meself, ar.'
'Good for the bowels, yea.'
'She cuddent see nuffin, nar.'
'But now we ain't got no garden.'

Alexandra Park. Scaffolding up nineteen years before the View Bar, a worker in overalls cleaning, as if combing, a stone lion's mane. In the ballroom the middle-aged tango on Sundays. A giant building-crane moving its head like a praying mantis in the misted valley below the pitch-and-putt course where early morning golfers move. Painted on the wall below the roller-skating rink: PUKE ON THE DUKE.

'Ta-ta Lew. See you then.'

Departure after four days. Night flight. From 25,000 feet the dinginess below is hidden, replaced by lines of glowing orange fire mixed with electric green and blue, topaz and emerald, all that can be seen of sodium-arc flares, the long motorways, oval arenas of the soccer stadiums that infest the land, the false moon identified as a navigation light on the aft wing. Leaving behind, *Jesus Christ Superstar*, still running at Cambridge Circus, *The Mousetrap* into its twenty-sixth year, the faces of the damned in Leicester Square, the suicided nurse in the Women's Pond on the heath, the murdered defective youth (the Kentish Town Cowboys were suspected) in the Lido. The dark absence of being.

Modern cities have become *pissoirs*. Hippies piss in Gedächt-niskirche; about Bahnhof Zoo the very air is lewd.

They say you go to the zoo to see yourself in the animals. There aren't enough animals in the world to see ourselves in. (Bellow.)